# DATE DUE

|  |  |  |  |
|---|---|---|---|
|  |  |  |  |
|  |  |  |  |
|  |  |  |  |
|  |  |  |  |
|  |  |  |  |
|  |  |  |  |
|  |  |  |  |
|  |  |  |  |
|  |  |  |  |
|  |  |  |  |
|  |  |  |  |
|  |  |  |  |
|  |  |  |  |
|  |  |  |  |

# CRISIS
## CONTROL

To all those unknown men and women
who have managed crises.

# CRISIS
## CONTROL

■ Preventing & managing
corporate crises

Ross Campbell

PRENTICE HALL

Acquisitions Editor: Nella Soeterboek
Project Editor: Sarah Welling
Typeset by The Type Group, Wollongong, NSW
Printed in Australia by Australian Print Group, Maryborough, Vic.

1 2 3 4 5 03 02 01 00 99

ISBN 0 7248 0011 5

---

National Library of Australia
Cataloguing-in-Publication Data

---

Campbell, Ross
    Crisis Control: preventing and
    managing corporate crises

    Includes index,
    ISBN 0 7248 0011 5

    1. Crisis management.  2. Emergency management.
    3. Risk management.  4. Business planning.  I. Title.

---

658.4056

---

Every effort has been made to trace and acknowledge copyright.
However, should an omission have occurred, the publishers tender
their apologies and invite copyright owners to contact them.

PRENTICE HALL

# CONTENTS

# PREFACE

How often have we heard the expression 'this is completely out of control'? A crisis of any magnitude can hit an organisation where it hurts without a moment's notice and it doesn't take long to lose control. The only protection is a well-rehearsed crisis management plan.

In a matter of minutes, a serious incident or emergency can run out of control and seriously disrupt a business with catastrophic effect. In some cases, it takes years to recover.

The right response actions can minimise serious damage and can quickly put an organisation in control of its destiny. Management needs to consider the organisation strategically and ask, 'what is the worst thing that could possibly happen?'. Fire, financial problems, lawsuits, product defect, sexual harassment, act of violence, technology collapse, executive misconduct or environmental issues to name a few. With the most likely threats in mind, management can prepare strategies to avoid or manage a potential problem and control the agenda.

Reading between the lines in today's media reports of crises, it is easy to see which organisations have anticipated the problem and have a planning process in place to deal with it. If an organisation is ready, then there will be a clear message about what is being done and who is doing it.

It is not just large organisations that need to have comprehensive and integrated crisis management plans. It is equally important that small and medium-sized organisations look at their worst case scenarios. The service industry, local government, educational institutions, professional firms and research organisations all need crisis plans. They often face the greatest damage from a negative event because they may lack the financial and managerial support required to respond and recover efficiently.

Ownership of crisis management planning must come from the top because most crises end up at the top. Our best executives recognise that crisis management is a corporate governance strategy and endorse its implementation. They know that a crisis out of control is liable to lead to loss of profits, lawsuits, loss of market share, serious loss of reputation and, in many cases, loss of senior jobs. After writing numerous plans for organisations, I am totally convinced that unless complete support of the Chief Executive and top management is assured, the crisis management program will flounder and never reach its full potential. The day the Chief Executive endorses the organisation's intentions to install a crisis management program is the day it really happens.

The best example of being out of control is to look at what happens during a car accident. Two vehicles collide and, for the first few minutes, the drivers and occupants (hopefully without injury) tend to wander around in circles considering the problem and attempting to deal with it. It is often not until emergency services arrive on the scene that trained personnel take control of the situation. Decision-making time is reduced and due to the emergency services' prior experience, performance and response improves and the situation is brought under control.

This is very much the same process in crisis management. Response teams need to be trained in a number of critical disciplines so they are armed with the capability and authority to make decisions. Training is essential and this book lays emphasis on regular training for teams so that each member understands exactly what to do and how to do it.

The simple questions I would ask any organisation related to crisis management are:

- what is the worst case scenario that could hit your organisation?
- what is the most inconvenient time for this to happen?
- do you have a plan to deal with it?
- who will lead your response?
- can you contact your key stakeholders rapidly?
- where will you manage the response from?
- have you identified ways of continuing to run your business?
- what are your short-term and long-term recovery goals?

*Crisis Control* should bring into sharp focus specific guidelines that are appropriate for managing a crisis and answering these questions.

Unfortunately, no crisis management book can offer the ultimate response plan because there are so many unknowns and unintended possibilities. This book offers a number of tried and tested suggestions and case studies. Where possible, the book identifies simple strategies and checklists for making efficient response decisions.

In closing this preface, there are some important people to thank in the preparation of this book. Firstly, Dr Michael Hewitt-Gleeson for the idea. My knowledge was enlarged by dealing with crisis events in the field and working with my partner and brother, Euan Campbell and colleagues John Barth and Warren Thompson. Ray Fisher helped considerably with the research and Rochelle Schetzer compiled the manuscript. My thanks go to the number of clients who have entrusted me with both their response work and crisis management planning, which led to the development of a number of strategic processes. Fitzroy Boulting managed the project and Nella Soeterboek from Pearson Education Australia (formerly Prentice Hall) made it happen. Finally, my family, Penny, Hugh and Sarah who are, in their own way, experienced crisis managers after living with the progress of this book.

Ross Campbell

'*The human crisis is always a crisis of understanding:
what we genuinely understand we can do.*'

Raymond Williams, academic and author (1921–88)
*Culture and Society*

# FOREWORD

Hardly a day goes by without some crisis making news headlines. Whatever the nature of the crisis—financial, health or natural disaster to name but a few—the common feature is that people, sometimes many people, are adversely affected. Crisis news travels fast and in this age of technology, the bigger the crisis, the faster and more global the impact.

A crisis that is badly handled by the organisation concerned invariably produces condemnation from the public at large as well as stakeholders, government and the media. This is often coupled with feelings of anger and hostility. If not managed carefully, the damage to an organisation as a result of a major crisis can be devastating, even terminal, not to mention the increased opportunities for protracted litigation.

Sometimes the view is put forward that since a crisis cannot be anticipated or predicted, particularly with regard to its timing, it cannot be planned for or controlled. This is entirely fallacious. Whilst we may not be able to predict a particular crisis, an essential element of risk management is to determine (plan) in advance what, when and how to deal with an unforeseen disastrous event or crisis when it occurs. Indeed, the modern organisation must be flexible and able to accommodate constant change.

Crisis management is now an important part of strategic management because it enables an organisation to reduce the threats and vulnerabilities related to a crisis.

This book advocates that organisations become committed to crisis management as part of good corporate governance and accountability. It also suggests that crisis management becomes a key performance indicator for managers in their strategic role and that the process of crisis planning, preparation and education be subject to continual improvement.

The introduction of new courses in university curricula is often a good indicator of emerging trends in society. We have recently seen the introduction into university curricula of studies in international business, electronic commerce, change management, management of information systems, including issues of security and privacy, and crisis management. In addition to students of management learning about successful business strategies based on an unchanging landscape, it is important for future managers to have a solid understanding of ways to cope with risks, threats and crises.

This book focuses on a key issue for *any* organisation. No organisation, board or chief executive can afford not to have a crisis management and recovery plan in place. Ross Campbell provides a brilliant, lucid and readable account of all aspects of crisis management planning and recovery. Practical, proven solutions are offered to a wide range of critical situations. I am confident that very few of those who read the preface to this book and/or glance at its contents pages, will be able to put it down before reading it from cover to cover.

I congratulate Ross on providing a much needed text on a topic whose importance cannot be overstated. His many years of experience as a crisis management consultant to some of Australia's largest organisations is evident throughout. I commend the book to all leaders and managers who take their responsibilities seriously.

Professor John Rickard
Pro-Vice Chancellor and Dean
Faculty of Business and Economics
Monash University

# 1

# THE CRISIS IMPERATIVE

It is 3.30 a.m. and a dull, crimson glow throbs on the black horizon. The CEO looks hard across the city at his plant—one of the world's biggest. The company boasts leadership in its field. He is now wide awake. Fifteen minutes ago, his General Manager Operations was on the telephone: 'There's been an explosion. It's blown half the site out and some of our people have been killed.' He can see the empty freeway filling now with countless emergency vehicles—the flashing blue, orange and red lights trailing towards the city in a morbid celebration. Both his home and mobile telephones are ringing. The leak of deadly gas is spreading to the many crowded cottages surrounding the plant. This is the crisis they said would not happen here.

How typical is this scenario? A successful corporation. A known brand. Now faced with a catastrophe that in just a few hours could reach the magnitude of an international disaster. The nature and the scale of the problem are almost impossible to recover from. There are very few, if any, strategic options. And while their corporate business planning and marketing processes are the most sophisticated, the decision-making plan to save its soul may have been left too late.

Sounds like the *Titanic*, doesn't it? Echoes of Bhopal. Memories of the *Challenger* space mission. A stark reminder of the *Exxon Valdez* oil tanker. There is a familiar ring—a fatal flaw in response planning.

It is astonishing, and ultimately unforgivable come the day, how many businesses and other organisations still say 'It can't happen here'. Generally, we live in a society that does not discuss crisis. The 'It can't happen here' syndrome is everywhere. Too many organisations are simply not prepared for the worst. So it comes as a painful shock when they are confronted by a crisis head-on. Inevitably, they can neither manage the situation, nor cope with the consequences.

Yet, it takes years to build a successful organisation, and it takes only minutes for a crisis to pull it apart. And, while it is a fact of life that success does not happen overnight, the corollary is that failure often does. Massive damage can be done to corporate reputation, sometimes for ever.

Considerable damage was done to the company Anglo American's reputation in South Africa after a crisis accident that caused horrific death and injuries and attracted international media attention. In what the press described as South Africa's worst mining disaster for almost a decade, a runaway train used to carry men, equipment and ore underground, ran off the rails and fell on a lift cage, killing 105 people. There were no survivors.

The freak accident occurred at Anglo American Corporation's Vaal Reefs goldmine in South Africa in May 1995. Anglo American is the largest mining company in the country. The mine is located in Orkney, 150 km south of Johannesburg. Most of the men killed in the accident were migrant workers from Mozambique, Lesotho and Malawi.

The disaster occurred when a government inquiry into mine safety was already in progress. President Nelson Mandela is quoted as 'promising swift action on [the] coming government report on mine safety'. From the company's point of view, the timing seemed likely to intensify media and public scrutiny of the accident. President Mandela also announced an immediate inquiry into the Vaal Reefs disaster.

Points to emerge were the need to be prepared for unpredictable as well as predictable crises, and the importance of controlling media access to company personnel. The suggestion that workers at the mine had been gagged provided a focus for media attention and was highly damaging to the company.

At the time of the first reports, the cause of the accident was unclear and the driver of the train—who had leapt to safety before the crash—had yet to be interviewed. However, claims of negligence and of South Africa's poor safety standards in mines, and calls for an independent inquiry, were already appearing. These came chiefly from union leaders. Mining analysts were quoted as predicting grave repercussions for the image of the industry.

2

The accident occurred when the train and a carriage, parked 1.7 km underground, were set in motion and bypassed safety devices before plunging into the lift shaft. The train fell 100 m before striking the cage, which was pushed 500 m down the shaft by the impact.

The mine's general manager, Mr Dick Fisher, said the train should have gone into neutral and stopped when the driver left it and he 'could not understand why this had not happened'. He claimed the steel safety blocks which should have halted the train had been there 'last week' but were missing at the time of the accident. Mr Fisher was the only company spokesperson quoted in local news reports at the time of the accident.

The Vaal Reefs mine disaster shook the country. President Mandela declared a national day of mourning. The Minister for Minerals and Energy, Mr Pik Botha, visited the mine and his vivid and emotive accounts of the scene were extensively quoted.

Nothing tests an organisation's survival as much as a crisis, because a crisis is unusual, unnatural, unforgiving and, at times, unknown.

Nobody in their personal life, in most cases, is prepared for a sudden trip to the hospital in the middle of the night; a car smash on the way to the office; a flooded home in summer; or a robbery or a violent attack. It is human nature to avoid these things. But, ask those who have been through personal crisis. They have learnt ways and means of dealing with the situation. They have some idea of what to do next time, who to call or what to say, how to respond and manage the situation. Business, on the other hand, does have the time, the resources and the financial and legal imperatives to learn beforehand, to plan ahead.

The *Exxon Valdez* oil spill off the coast of Alaska in 1989 is still referred to as one of the worst environmental disasters in US history, but it also was an example of complex failures in emergency planning and a failure of crucial communications to a wide range of audiences.

By contrast, Greenhill Petroleum responded to rapidly shifting public values and rising expectations of the oil industry by dealing with a much smaller spill in a highly efficient way. In September 1992, Greenhill Petroleum, drilling in Timbalier Bay in Louisiana, experienced a 'blowout' at one of its 100 wells in the course of a routine operation, and spilt oil into the Gulf of Mexico. Workers on the platform had to leap to safety as the oil ignited. There were injuries but no fatalities.

The oil spill and subsequent fire, occurring in a sensitive marine environment, was potentially threatening to the reputation of the company and was reported throughout the United States, from the Louisiana media to the *Los Angeles Chronicle* and the *Wall Street Journal*.

It was also the first major oil pollution crisis since the passing of the stringent US Oil Pollution Act of 1990, known as OPA 90, which was the result of the *Exxon Valdez* oil spill in Alaska. Since the law was passed, equipment has been installed along the US coastlines to contain oil spills. Spill containment equipment was in place in New Orleans at the time of the Greenhill spill.

Under the terms of the Oil Pollution Act, petroleum companies in the United States are required to have a crisis management plan in place. The manual must be lodged with the relevant Federal agency for examination and approval, and be updated annually to comply with regulations.

Company personnel are required to take part in regular training drills conducted by the US Federal agency on how to respond to an oil spill. These may take the form of 'tabletop' or actual field operations.

In addition to this government-approved manual, Greenhill had an internal company plan which it considered more concise, practicable and readily implementable. The handbook set out in detail step-by-step procedures to be followed by each corporate division. It also listed contact numbers of all resources, including contractors and government agencies, who might require to be contacted in the event of a crisis.

Immediately the spill was reported, Greenhill implemented a two-phase operation to put out the fire and control the spill.

Specifically, it took these measures:

- It informed the relevant government agencies including the coastguard, with whom it then worked in close co-operation.
- A core team of six to seven personnel, including engineers and geologists, moved to the field to be as close as possible to the scene of the accident. This group later followed the coastguard to a new location at Fourchon on the Louisiana coast.
- Boots and Cootes, one of the three largest oil well firefighting companies in the world, was called in to put out the fire at the wells.
- Industrial Clean Up was subcontracted to help clean up the spill.

The team's day began at 7.00 a.m. Each day it was required to hand to the coastguard a plan of the next day's operations, for revision and approval.

Greenhill made the decision to handle media liaison in-house. From the outset of the crisis:

4

- News was updated every two to three hours and news releases despatched all round the country to industry publications, as well as to the general media.
- The company President—who was experienced in media liaison and a master of the 'sound bite'—became the chief spokesperson and gave interviews to the press and electronic media at Greenhill's New Orleans office at Metarie.
- The media was closely monitored and any misinformation corrected quickly in new releases.

As part of its overall strategy, the Spill Response Team also:

- called in the organisation International Bird Rescue to work with the company (this defused potential flack from environmentalists and 'good PR' resulted from this care of affected birds, which was picked up and reported in the media);
- set up telephone lines, which families and friends of personnel on the rigs could ring for up-to-date information; and
- equipped personnel on the wells with cellular telephones so they could easily contact family and friends.

Since its 1992 oil spill, Greenhill has reviewed and revised its Oil Spill Contingency Plan. The handbook has been developed further, and the team expanded and broken down into smaller groups.

As well as oil spills, the company's crisis management plan provides for other contingencies such as hurricanes. The course of the Greenhill oil spill crisis bears out the importance of having an effective crisis management plan in place, and the ability to implement it. Instead of incurring huge fines, Greenhill was commended by Federal agencies including the powerful US coastguard.

According to a company spokesperson, throughout the ten-day course of the crisis, 'communication—with federal agencies, the media, interest groups and families of company personnel—was the No. 1 priority'.


## LEARNING THE HARD WAY

In the 1980s, organisations were faced with an increasing need to protect their reputations. Crisis management became a catchphrase after the *Exxon Valdez* oil spill at Prince William Sound in Alaska, the Piper Alpha oil rig explosion in the North Sea, the Union Carbide chemical release at Bhopal in India, and cases of product tampering, such as Tylenol analgesics.

The 1990s have seen a new and more intense focus on crisis symptoms and on essential plans of action to be implemented quickly once a negative situation occurs. Crisis management has evolved into a vital tool of business management, and is increasingly on the agendas of CEOs and the boards of those companies concerned about reputation.

The debate between the Chairman and CEO of the Shell Oil Company and Greenpeace over the Brent Spar oil rig in the United Kingdom in 1995 was corporate theatre played to an international audience. Shell initially ignored the demands of Greenpeace, and then, in a complete turnaround, virtually agreed to all of them. Following that incident, Shell placed an advertisement in many newspapers and magazines. Even now, it is a target for campaigners who are calling for a halt to the company's activities in Nigeria.

For Dow Corning, its silicone breast implant has been one of the most expensive class actions in US history, occupying the minds and profits of the company for several years. The CEO and board faced the severest public criticism over its management of the escalating issue.

One of Australia's largest companies, mining giant BHP, faced a plethora of crises from the 1980s into the 1990s. These included a tragic underground explosion, which killed 14 miners and led to the closure of the mine involved; an oil spill off the coast of Tasmania, which threatened the state's environment; and the death of two workers in a steel plant.

More recently, the company has been besieged by lawyers and conservationists over alleged pollution to a river at the Ok Tedi mine in Papua New Guinea, which seemed to come down to a political trade-off—economic advantage to the nation versus damage to the local environment. All these events created a groundswell of dissatisfaction with BHP, in a very public way at its Annual General Meeting.

And, of course, in 1992 and 1993, two of the City of London's oldest and most respected institutions, Lloyds and Barings, faced colossal financial disasters. These almost unthinkable crises rocked the very foundation of the City establishment. Lloyds was left with massive human, legal and financial problems, while Barings has been bought at a bargain basement price by an overseas company. Crises at the top, from the top.

The tragic TWA air disaster came at a time when increased scrutiny had been placed on organisations to show how their crisis management planning works. The incident covered the front pages of US and international publications for months—television news cameras searched every scientific, academic and social expert for comment. The affected public went into severe shock and, eventually, fury.

6

The next of kin of the 230 passengers and crew heading for Paris on that TWA flight went through sheer hell, as they waited to hear the latest news. TWA was castigated on the US Channel 7 'Eyewitness News' when their planning and communication was criticised as being 'woefully inadequate'. The real problem was lack of information. Control of the story was taken over by the media. This allowed rumour and innuendo to run rife.

In 1996 one of Australia's worst crises in food products occurred. The manufacturer, Kraft, owned by General Foods Ltd, withdrew its entire stock of peanut butter as a result of an outbreak of salmonella poisoning. The company faced severe criticism for its failure to communicate adequately in the early days of the recall.

The issues were led by a broad range of commentators because of an initial lack of adequate spokespeople and confusion about which brands had been withdrawn. The Managing Director of Kraft did not make an appearance as spokesperson until much later in the incident. Messages were confusing and brand integrity was questioned by many stake-holders and, in particular, by the most essential consumers, children.

General Foods Ltd Australia faced a multi-million dollar compensation payout to food poisoning victims and lawyers advertised in the media to communicate with those persons who believed they might have suffered injuries and required assistance in making claims.

The massive weight of publicity surrounding legal action can bring a company, and a brand, to its knees (see Figure 1.1). Litigation action is big news, as we have seen from the thousands of claims on the insulation material, asbestos, also on the intrauterine birth control device, the Dalkon Shield, silicone breast implants and pacemakers.

*Figure 1.1* Headline re Kraft food crisis from The Age, *27 June 1996, p.1.*

# Food giant's crisis recall

## The corporate crisis

Crisis management deserves top positioning on the corporate menu, for any number of reasons. Class action lawsuits are up; directors' liability is high on the legal agenda; insurance premiums are growing; environmental investigations are intense and constant; urban terrorism is spreading; and media scrutiny of business scandals is front page news.

The threat of a company being badly managed is also on the crisis agenda. The President of the World Bank, Jim Wolfensohn, has asserted that corporate honesty will become as crucial to the world economy as the proper governing of countries.

Crisis makes us smarter. They make us fix things that we knew were wrong but were too busy to mend. As the battered economies of the emerging markets piece themselves back together in 1999, one lesson will not be forgotten: rotten national economies spring from rotten corporations; if business life is not run on open and honest lines, there is little chance that the wider economy can be.

Wolfensohn, J. *The Economist 1998 Year in Review*

## The road to recovery

There is a recent addition to strategic thinking in crisis management. Because of the many failed crisis responses of the 1980s, there is a greater focus on recovery and business resumption. Insurance companies and risk managers have included these factors in the crisis equation to minimise disruptions, to maintain control and to assure recovery. What will it take to recover assets and earnings? How long will it take to clean up the mess? How will it deal with the traumatic effect on people, on the environment, and on the day-to-day operation of the business?

Recovery planning ensures minimal disruption of operations and continuing organisation control in crisis. An organisation that is geared for business continuity already has planning in place to secure its gross profit under any circumstances. While business continuity can be affected by a number of intangible hazards, such as market shift or exchange rates, the primary goal of recovery planning is to increase the likelihood of survival in the event of physical hazards, both man-made and natural, that have the potential to destroy or damage the business.

8

# GROUND ZERO—THE TYRANNY OF TIME

Crises can come at any time, usually out of nowhere. They come at different speeds, from different delivery systems, and, in many cases, do not follow normal working hours. Many of the world's worst disasters have occurred at night. Holidays are particularly popular for crises related to chemical spills, plant accidents and fires. One of Australia's worst disasters, a cyclone that destroyed much of the city of Darwin, occurred on Christmas Day, 1974.

It is amazing how many nightwatchmen become corporate spokespersons when a disaster occurs on the night-time watch at large industrial plants. Equally, it comes as no surprise how few nightwatchmen are trained to face the barrage of questions from media, neighbours, environmentalists and others following a negative event. This nightwatchman is often the only person available for comment in the first 30 minutes of a site disaster after hours.

In what is now recognised as a benchmark case study in crisis management for Johnson & Johnson and their analgesic product, Tylenol, time moved tragically fast. Two mothers, two sisters, a young married woman, a 12-year old schoolgirl and a flight attendant did as millions of people do every day, and reached for their standard painkiller. They all died very quickly of cyanide poisoning from the most vicious kind of product tampering.

The message spread from Chicago right across the United States. Twenty-one percent of all evening television news and huge newspaper, magazine and radio coverage saw to that. The media coverage grew to be given more space and time than any other story since the assassination of President John F. Kennedy. The public was terrified.

There was no time for longwinded strategy meetings or qualitative and quantitative research, the crisis was there and the manufacturer had to act. But the company had a plan, and that plan was in place *before* its worst nightmare hit. Their timing was critical.

Johnson & Johnson, the makers of Tylenol, went against its advisers and recalled everything. The company worked with the Federal Drug Administration (FDA), and, at a cost of more than $US150 million, developed a tamper-resistant package for the redistribution of its product. Brand loyalty was restored and market share reclaimed, even in the face of copycat tampering activity.

It is impossible to avoid all risks, but it is your right and, indeed, your responsibility to consider how to deflect threats, as well as prepare for the worst case scenarios. By including the risk factors in planning,

9

we anticipate and are prepared for the real world, where the probability of damage to life, property and the environment will occur.

Real security comes from self-sufficiency, and the best form of crisis management comes from being prepared to manage the first few minutes and hours at the crisis location. This is, after all, where the focus of the event is, where the greatest impact will be, where the media will head, and where the serious issues will be tackled.

## THE NAME GAME— THE DEFINITION OF CRISIS

Because crisis management and recovery is a relatively new corporate discipline, management is continually debating the most suitable title. Some organisations prefer the title of disaster. Others believe that the word catastrophe is an excellent word for the super-crisis. The media, of course, use the word crisis in news and current affairs at an ever-increasing rate. Crisis can be a subeditor's best friend. The word is short and the meaning is clear.

*Figure 1.2* Escalation control chart

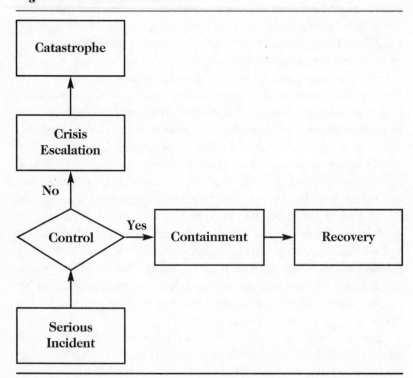

There are many theories and concepts about which word is best to describe a serious, negative event that has detrimental effects on an organisation. Crisis sits best with me, because I believe it has been accepted by the majority of large international organisations as an essential part of their corporate agenda.

The nomenclature crisis management has certainly found a place in modern enterprises where a process needs to be established for dealing with a serious, negative event. A number of academic institutions in the United States and United Kingdom have established undergraduate and postgraduate courses in crisis management, and it is encouraging that so many business groups and universities have now set up centres for crisis management research and study.

So, what about emergency management? When does an emergency become a crisis? These questions are often asked by industrial manufacturing, chemical, petroleum and mining industries. Some emergencies will never become a crisis.

Others are a crisis from the start. A small fire in a plant can be classified as an emergency, but if that fire spreads and engulfs a building containing dangerous chemicals or gases, resulting in a large explosion which kills or injures employees and virtually wipes out the plant, then the emergency is a crisis.

While there is a danger of theories which oversimplify the definition of emergency and crisis, they are distinctly different management areas.

An emergency is a sudden, usually unexpected occurrence that requires immediate response from either internal or external emergency services. Emergency management is, therefore, the development of an effective incident response system that focuses on controlling the event.

A crisis is an adverse incident, or series of events, that has the potential to seriously damage an organisation's employees, operations, business and reputation.

How is crisis best defined? Ian I. Mitroff, Christine M. Pearson and L. Catherine Harrrington in their book *The Essential Guide to Managing Corporate Crisis* (1996) refer to a crisis across a broad range of areas.

A crisis can affect the very existence of an organisation, a major product line, a business unit, or the like. A crisis also can damage, perhaps severely, an organisation's financial performance. A crisis can also harm the death and well-being of consumers, employees, the surrounding community and the environment itself. Finally, a crisis can destroy the public's basic trust or belief in an organisation, its reputation and its image.

11

While the word 'crisis' can be described, as the dictionary puts it, as: 'a decisive moment or a turning point', Steve Albrecht, ex-San Diego policeman and now US crisis and security consultant, in his book *Crisis Management for Corporate Self Defense* defines crisis as: 'A business-based crisis is an event-specific episode that can make or break you, depending upon the size of your company, the number of people you employ, the products and services you sell, and the resources or people, assets and money you can aim at the problem.'

If you are determining your organisation's current level of preparedness for dealing with a crisis, it is important to recognise that emergency management will certainly prepare you for the essential elements of technical and tactical response in fighting fires, chemical spills, injuries to employees and similar incidents.

But emergency management, in most cases, does not deal with the corporate issues, such as protecting the company's reputation by managing external sources of enquiry from government, community, media and interest groups.

It does not provide a safety net for the security of shareholders, nor demonstrate the completeness of management's planning for business resumption and recovery.

Crisis management, as distinct from emergency management, is about assuring shareholders and stakeholders that management is in control of the situation and the future of the business is secure.

Crisis management has to be a culture of its own, with a clear focus on corporate control and the protection of the company's assets. It cannot be dominated by an overemphasis on an emergency services driven culture, a security culture, or a safety culture. Neither should crisis management be driven by a public relations process. If, for example, crisis planning is ruled by quick-fix solutions in a media-influenced, tell-it-fast approach, incorrect messages can serve to escalate, not control, the crisis.

Dynamic crisis management uses a balanced mix of tactics involving threat analysis, crisis preparation, crisis containment with business continuity and recovery.

## THE THREAT FROM WITHIN — THE BUSINESS CRISIS

Most of the well-publicised crises fall into the category of environmental catastrophes, product tampering, weather-related incidents and major accidents. The crime of extortion is growing throughout the world. Health problems in international capital cities are dominating news, as infrastructures strain under the weight of growing populations. Technology and computer problems are heading up risk management agendas. There is, however, a growing recognition of corporate and business-related crises caused by organisational action or inaction. The risks for organisations today are more complex than ever, and many of these risks threaten business profitability and survival.

An organisation can have a well-orchestrated crisis plan for dealing with the escalation of emergencies or a product recall, and yet still face ruin from a business scandal.

Premier organisations throughout the world are experiencing the heat of public scrutiny on how their businesses are run. There are major regulatory issues facing the capital markets predicting new implications and repercussions. Shareholders and financial markets are asking more questions about corporate integrity, governance, ethics, private gain and conflict of interest. Just consider how many business-related crises start in the financial pages of newspapers and end up as front-page news.

A complex web of corporate governance issues and board dealings moved Coles Myer, one of Australia's largest chain of department stores, from the finance pages to the front pages, in what has been one of the longest running corporate crises in Australia's history. In 1995, its Chief Financial Officer, Mr Philip Bowman, made allegations about boardroom impropriety after he was sacked. Shares were rapidly slashed by 6% and the stock continued to drop.

In 1993, in what was considered to be the world's worst factory fire at the Kader plant in Bangkok, Thailand, 188 workers died and more than 400 were injured. The financial pages in Asia led many of the stories on the company's business responsibility. Thailand's Prime Minister was quoted as saying to the company: 'How could you let this happen?'.

Every CEO, every corporate head office, must be concerned about the effect of a business crisis on the reputation of the company or organisation. Flexible procedures for dealing with a range of potential crisis situations can be so easily introduced, and can so easily help avoid misinformation, rumour mongering, shareholder panic, institutional loss of support, loss of confidence and other disastrous effects on the bottom line.

If an organisation is faced with any of the following issues, it will in some way need a crisis management plan:

- business scandal
- senior executive resignation or termination
- government investigation
- bankruptcy
- lay-offs
- hostile takeover
- loss of vital information
- major reorganisation or merger
- regulatory changes
- abrupt market changes
- criticism of corporate governance.

Of course, the aim of business is to do as much as possible to prevent any of these situations happening in the first place, but you cannot contain damage unless you have a plan.

Business rumours move fast. Sophisticated communications and media networks, fast information technology systems, competitors seeking a business edge, leak-prone governments and human nature make sure of that. But often, they are the wrong messages, sending the wrong signals. Stage managing and controlling the corporate communications agenda is high on the priority of crisis preparedness.

Similarly, any international business crisis plan needs to look at the effect of time zones, financial market operating times, financial and news media deadlines and their own corporate response capability within those time parameters.

## THINKING AHEAD—THE CRITICAL SUCCESS FACTORS

The crisis you do not expect or plan for will be the one that is likely to cause the most damage. And while a lot of pundits believe that a good manager is automatically a good crisis manager, it is important to understand that many managers cannot cope with the stress, pressure and abnormal behaviour that occurs during a crisis. Most normal management behaviour is reversed. One minute you are managing a business, the next minute you have to manage a crisis. Different skills under different pressures. How many managers can move rapidly from the normal pace of a business meeting to the hectic, urgent demanding pace of life and death decisions, evacuation, emotional trauma and split-second timing?

Containment is the key. Managers who are prepared, rehearsed, educated, trained and aware are those that can make the transition when crisis hits and contain the situation.

If there is a single, critical feature to being prepared for crisis, it is in treating crisis management and recovery as an ongoing process. Seeing it as an integral part of the company's everyday business activities, not merely as a plan that is created, approved, then shelved until needed.

It is a process that has the whole company—from site management to CEO and board—trained, tested and involved in a crisis management plan that is integrated seamlessly across the whole organisation. This process has to be regularly monitored, reviewed and audited, just like any other quality control policy that is demanded by compliance factors in today's business environment.

To achieve this, there are a number of critical features of a crisis plan that facilitate speedy business resumption. Whether the crisis is an oil and chemical spill or explosion, a tainted food product or charges of business corruption, a crisis management and recovery plan must:

- have tactical decisions made at the crisis location, and quickly (this is where the public focus will be initially);
- localise the response, while maximising corporate and strategic assistance;
- provide training and support to give staff the skills and confidence so they can manage the early stages of a crisis, and back them up with appropriate technology;
- create a tailor-made plan around uniform standards throughout the company;
- develop realistic simulation and training exercises;
- start planning for recovery before a crisis occurs; and
- instil a company-wide recognition of the potential impact of a crisis.

What fundamentally distinguishes crisis-prepared, from crisis-prone organisations, is their overall cultural view of crisis management and recovery.

Strategic actions, technical and structural response, communication initiatives and psychological support have to be part of an integrated management plan and process that immediately puts the organisation in charge of its own destiny. This process must be a corporate package of total commitment by its staff and executives to customers, shareholders and general public.

# THE BENEFITS ARE ALL BOTTOM LINE

Having a crisis management and recovery plan in place offers an organisation a number of immediate benefits. In short, these are:

- increased awareness of exposure to crises;
- understanding of the full range of issues likely to be encountered;
- a plan specifically configured to each operation and business unit;
- improved crisis communication between management, employees, media, government, suppliers and customers;
- company employees that better understand their roles and responsibilities, their strengths and weaknesses, and their part in the bigger picture; and
- enhanced corporate governance, management control and an improved reputation with external opinion makers such as government, bankers, financial analysts and industry peers.

The ultimate benefit of a crisis plan is the capability given to managers and staff to retain effective control of any situation as a direct result of their own planning and training. This ensures that employees and third parties, assets and earnings, the environment and corporate reputation remain as safe and secure as possible.

# THE PROCESS OF CRISIS PLANNING— BEFORE, DURING AND AFTER

Much crisis planning tends to be fairly fatalistic. In other words, it offers crisis managers a plan to only deal with 'what happens if'.

This plan proposes more than the inevitable. It sets out a process for superior performance in lead time, analysis of threats and wider response into recovery.

A crisis plan cannot be based on a standard set of critical decisions that determine specific success. The plan must be flexible and able to cope with a broad range of crisis types. Crisis basically is a non-routine event and the ability of an organisation to hone in on a versatile response is a key determinant of attainment. Organisations that know what is going to happen before it happens, who is going to do what and in what sequence, will leap ahead in any critical path. Flexibility and capability, with prior authorisation and authority, will lead to a single-minded sense of purpose and cohesion.

16

*Figure 1.3* Crisis process continual improvement

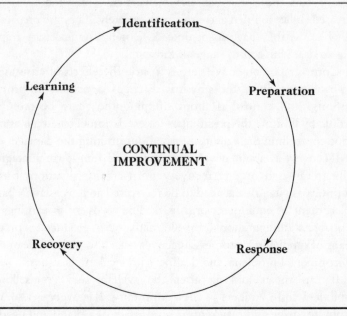

The following stages establish a flexible process (see Figure 1.3):

* Identification/discovery

  Before
* Preparation/planning
* Response/control    During
* Recovery

  After
* Learning

Identification or discovery of threats is a skill most organisations have, but under-utilise. This is because determining the imminent approach of a crisis is often difficult when managers and front-line employees are faced with an endless array of information.

The organisation may not be trained to listen to employees or customers who signal problems and issues. They may not identify the significance of a technical defect or a business rumour. These issues equate to a lost opportunity for prevention, or wasted time in which to act positively before the onset of crisis.

Preparation and planning can be increased by a number of activities, ranging from threat and vulnerability audits, identification of emerging issues, safety inspections, emergency planning, improved relationships with employees and external audiences, even by media training. When a crisis occurs, those organisations which are crisis-prepared have a much increased ability to listen and to act appropriately. They are prepared for crisis because they have spent time developing the necessary response plans to deal with a wide range of threats.

Control. The objective here is to stop the effects of crisis as soon as possible, to limit the physical damage to people or property. Response and control is about stopping the acute becoming the chronic by limiting the possibilities for escalation. This step is as much about controlling the agenda as it is about limiting the damage.

Recovery is about developing short and long-term strategies to facilitate fast and orderly recovery from a crisis situation. Business continuity is vital. Assets need to be recovered and necessary repairs or replacement of equipment organised. The recovery of earnings may incorporate finding short-term alternatives for production or other means of supplying customers. Recovery can also include cleaning up environmental problems and dealing with legal implications.

It can mean looking after the welfare and counselling of employees and members of the community. Recovery is also about corporate image and may require a relaunch of a brand and product.

Learning is an ongoing process. It consists of understanding the crisis management plan and its checklists and procedures and continually reviewing the threats to the organisation and the crisis response. Learning also includes an evaluation of crisis from a wide range of sources and providing quality assurance and ongoing improvement and maintenance across the plan.

In terms of crisis planning, the five phases can be simplified into the three stages of *before*, *during* and *after*. The before stage is crisis planning, gaining company-wide awareness and preparedness and setting roles and responsibilities—all those initiatives which limit the possibility of crisis, warn of its onset, or, if it hits, limit its affect and duration. During is the activation of those plans and responses, and the after stage is aimed towards implementing business recovery strategies, and integrating any lessons learnt into the updated crisis plan.

## Prevention is not the best cure

In the ideal world, commentators suggest most crises can be prevented. Some crises can be prevented and there are many tried and tested solutions in place to achieve the ultimate status. Better warning systems, improved safety standards, regular risk and threat analysis, strategic issues management, best practice emergency and security standards—all contribute to reducing and in some cases eliminating crisis.

Real certainty seldom exists. Crises will erupt to disrupt and destabilise an organisation. While everything and everyone needs to be aware of prevention, it is not the cure for crisis. There is no cure. But one thing is certain—a crisis planning process can protect an organisation and control the chaos.

---

## CONTROL POINTS

☐ It takes years to build a successful organisation and only minutes to pull it apart.

☐ Be prepared for the unpredictable as well as predictable crisis.

☐ Crisis management needs top positioning on the corporate agenda.

☐ Focus on recovery and business resumption in planning.

☐ Corporate reputation and business threats need to be identified in addition to accidents, issues and product problems.

☐ Containment is the key. Managers who are prepared and rehearsed can contain faster.

☐ Crisis management needs to be an ongoing process not just a plan.

☐ Be prepared in three stages. Before (identification and preparation); during (response control); after (recovery).

☐ Lessons learnt in crisis need to be incorporated in the plan.

---

# 2

# DIAGNOSIS

The risk management expert from the insurance broker had identified a number of risk exposures. Nobody had expected two young female employees to charge the company with sexual harassment. Certainly no-one imagined this famous old firm would have to face months of front-page news, as the court case rambled on through witness after witness, many of them from the top row of executive managers. It was the court case from hell. If the company had taken responsibility instead of blaming others, it would have saved management from appearing irresponsible and inept. It would have reduced negative media coverage and may have saved its reputation. A case of sexual harassment was a threat that had never before been identified.

---

Planning for crisis begins with threat identification. It is about developing the ultimate hit list of possible threats that could affect your business and industry. It is more than just identifying insurance risks. It is about the anticipation of a broad range of threats and how serious the impact of each threat might be. This threat identification needs to be undertaken at least twice a year.

A good way to start is to consider any current areas of your operation that could present a serious threat to the bottom line. Build up a list of problems that might escalate into a crisis situation. Consider simple emergencies that, through changing circumstances, could develop into life-threatening, asset-threatening events. Look back at past crises that have taken place either in your business or in similar organisations. Anything that seriously affects the people who work for you, or the environment in which you operate, must be considered.

If one of your operating processes goes wrong and you become news or incite a government inquiry, then perhaps you may have a crisis on your hands.

The chance of these threats occurring needs to be qualified, but once you have established your threat hit list and the possible impact these threats may have on your operation or business, and if there is a high chance of these events occurring, then the threat of crisis is very real.

After what seemed to be a successful launch in January 1986, the US *Challenger* space shuttle exploded and disintegrated amidst clouds of smoke. The seven crew were killed instantly. The incident, viewed by millions of people around the world, had a particularly large audience of children because one of the astronauts was an American teacher.

The media was enthusiastic because they were watching this twenty-fifth space shuttle mission as an exciting space news story. The National Aeronautics and Space Administration (NASA) was poised to pass on the good news about another outstanding episode of space research history. NASA was not ready to deal with the bad news. Certainly they had a public affairs contingency plan in place for an accident emergency, but it was not up to speed. The threat of an accident was not the main priority.

It took too long to brief the media, the next of kin and the public. In the Rogers Commission Report to President Reagan, there was severe criticism of the NASA response:

For the first several days after the accident—possibly because of the trauma resulting from the accident—NASA appeared to be withholding information about the accident from the public. After the commission began its work, and at its suggestion, NASA began releasing a great deal of information that helped reassure the public that all aspects of the accident were being investigated and that the full story was being told in an orderly and thorough manner.

The possibility of a crisis for NASA had been considered as far back as 1983 when a contingency plan was put in place to deal with the public information issues related to a shuttle accident.

Then in one of the world's most public events, in the 1986 disastrous launch, NASA could not find a spokesperson to deal with the early crisis events. They were exposed in a very critical way for their inability to communicate essential information to a wide range of stakeholders.

The 1980s will be remembered for a number of critical crises that had a world-shattering effect—the *Challenger* explosion, Union Carbide's Bhopal, Chernobyl in the former USSR and the *Exxon Valdez* oil spill in Alaska. All of these crises happened quickly, without warning, and caused massive damage. None had really been planned for and the organisations involved had not clearly identified the vulnerability threat and prepared themselves with an appropriate response to deal with the situation.

In Australia's worst landslide in 1997, 20 people were entombed under tons of rock and soil at Thredbo ski holiday resort. This tragedy brought into play one of the largest emergency service rescues ever mounted in Australia, and miraculously one man survived this terror after 65 hours of sheer hell.

It was ten hours before the rescue operation began in earnest. This hold-up in rescue proceedings created a major debate between emergency services, as experts reviewed the instability of the hillside. Eight hours elapsed before contact was made with a geophysicist whose on-site assessment of the stability of the site was critical in determining when rescuers could start digging for survivors.

There is no doubt that rescue personnel were frustrated by the continued threat of further landslides and that this rescue was very dangerous for all emergency workers involved. This wait, of course, had a traumatic and horrendous emotional effect on relatives and friends of the landslide victims as they watched and waited on the edge of the site disaster scene.

Was the threat of a disastrous landslide ever identified by the management of the Thredbo ski resort? Australian ski rescuers are amongst the best in the world. Each Australian state boasts an outstanding emergency services and state disaster plan. Although one or two locals were concerned about the problem, most of the population of the sleeping village of Thredbo did not expect a fatal landslide on this steep slope. They did not expect water-laden top soil surging down a hillside, taking with it everything in its path.

Landslides are common in Europe. Alpine areas are inherently unstable because of their steep slopes and very young soil. Freezing and thawing can be a recipe for disaster. But still, the threat was not identified and therefore a crisis plan for such an event happening at Thredbo was not in place.

Threats need to be verified regularly. Crisis management is about proactively managing any organisation in such a way that the chances of crises occuring are minimised, and having plans in place so that a crisis can quickly be contained and controlled. And, it is about maintaining a positive attitude towards crisis management. No-one wants to live in an environment of impending danger and intimidation, but being prepared and having guidelines in place can make a world of difference in pinpointing the crisis for rapid response.

## THE TOP TEN NO-ONE WANTS TO HEAR

One of the more critical elements in beginning crisis planning is deciding what potential threats your organisation might face. Be careful to separate risks from threats. The threats in the crisis management process may not be the risks identified in risk management processes. Many threats—such as plant accidents and chemical spills—arise from an organisation's day-to-day activities, and come within the traditional province of risk management. However, your top crisis threat may be unrelated to your internal operations, involving loss of reputation or earnings due to an event caused by outside factors.

Risk management originated in the calculation of risks for insurance purposes. The responsibility of risks managers, who generally report to their company's financial controller, is to identify and evaluate operational risks, and manage them by buying appropriate insurance and putting in place management policies to minimise them —often in close collaboration with the company's insurer.

The risks an organisation faces are not a fixed quantity—risk must be continually reassessed. Risk assessment is essential when a new risk emerges, when the degree of existing risk changes or when a new perception of risk occurs. The emergence of new diseases, such as AIDS and CJD (Creutzfeldt Jakob Disease), has created new risks for the general community and the health sector—for example, the risk to blood banks of AIDS-contaminated blood.

Risk has always been associated with high political office, however the 1998 Monica Lewinsky scandal, which embroiled US President Bill Clinton, has redefined the degree and kind of risk. The ripple effects of this crisis continue to spread, with implications not only for the American presidency but for world financial markets and all governments affected by US foreign policy.

Organophosphates widely used in agriculture are now viewed with suspicion and have been banned from use in some countries. Today perceptions of risk attach to many other commonly used chemicals and food additives.

While risk management is chiefly interested in events that could impact negatively on a company's financial standing, the fallout from a crisis may be of a kind you could never put a dollar value on and may have no immediate consequences for the bottom line. In the 1980s in Australia, escalating Reserve Bank interest rates created a crisis of public confidence in the so called 'big banks'. Bank profits were not affected, but their image was. The crisis destroyed banks' privileged corporate status in the community. It made them much more vulnerable to criticism as well as to legal challenge by consumers. 'Bank bashing' has remained a popular public sport, with ongoing implications for banks on the levels of communication and policy.

It has been said that crisis and risk differ in that in a crisis the risks have been realised, and that crisis represents the failure of the risk management process.

However, a crisis can develop out of a threat that may never be identified in the process of risk assessment nor incur financial liability. For example, the private conduct of a highly placed staff member may attract adverse media attention and be forever associated with your company's name. Witness the series of sex scandals which have embroiled major political parties. Consider the untimely departure of many high profile CEOs after rumours about their unusual private lives have been made public.

On the other hand, while some risks, such as construction delays, may be potentially costly and central to a company's risk management program, they are unlikely to make the headlines in the daily press and embroil an organisation in crisis.

And the threat to an organisation through the escalation of an insurance risk into a crisis may go beyond what any risk manager could predict or cover. A recent case brought in Australia by a senior executive against her employer Westpac, a leading private bank, is a timely example. The woman claimed Westpac discriminated against her by demoting her after she was diagnosed with a terminal illness. The out-of-court settlement was no doubt covered by the company's insurers under its disability discrimination policy.

However, the damage to the bank's reputation as an employer and corporate citizen was not so easily repaired. And the media interest and public ill feeling had as much to do with the bank's poor reputational history as with the case itself. The Australian public's perception of banks as fair game also played a part in focusing attention on this particular case rather than on other comparable cases.

In other words, it is often the context and timing that determine the threat an event represents to a company's reputation.

Increasing government regulation, social change and the rise of special interest groups continue to create new threats which may run ahead of those recognised in traditional risk management practices. In the early 1990s, changing social attitudes and expectations led to the creation of a new form of insurance cover, Employment Practices Liability, to be introduced worldwide.

Sexual harassment, workplace discrimination and wrongful dismissal are amongst the risks covered by such policies. However, they were threats before they became insurance risks. And it could be argued that it was the media and public attention focused on specific instances of these behaviours that first put them on the agenda of risk managers and insurers.

Threats and risks can all give rise to crises. However, the spectrum of threats faced by an organisation is likely to be broader and more wide ranging than the risks identified in risk management. Threats may come from outside as well as within the organisation. They may threaten reputation more than profitability. And their crisis potential may stem as much from context and timing as from the events themselves.

In drawing up your list of crisis threats, establish the critical events most likely to occur, and determine the impact of these events on reputation, assets, earnings, personnel and their families, the environment, regulatory bodies and the local community.

The spectrum of corporate and operational crises is growing, as is the intensity of public scrutiny a crisis can attract to an organisation (see Figure 2.1). The more typical crises tend to be escalating emergencies and environmental accidents, a major security breach or a large evacuation. In a business sense, a hostile takeover, executive succession, vicarious liability or a financial problem can seriously affect a company's well-being and result in a crisis. A number of negative events can cause an organisation's loss of reputation, which is a crisis. As we saw with the Y2K bug, concern about an information technology (IT) loss can be a crisis. Health problems at home or abroad can destroy an organisation's well-being very quickly. Product recall can very often develop into a crisis for any manufacturing operation, particularly if sabotage is involved. There are many industrial relations actions that move into a prolonged crisis. And there is a wide range of critical issues related to different points of view that can grow into a dispute resulting in crisis.

Think about the top ten most serious potential crises your organisation could face, and why. Consider how well-prepared your

**Figure 2.1** *Typical corporate crisis threat field*

organisation would be if any of them happened in isolation or simultaneously. The impact should be measured in terms of financial cost, operational interruption *and* damage to reputation.

The threats can be identified by site audit or by workshops throughout all levels of the organisation, including executive management level (see Figure 2.2). Threats need to be listed according to their potential impact or magnitude (slight, moderate or severe), for probability of occurrence based on past experience and also by cost of damage to people, assets and reputation. By using this methodology, impact ratings can be analysed in order to diagnose ways to avoid some of these potential crises from happening. Often, actions can be put in place to reduce the severity of such threats.

Threats need to be reviewed often. As the organisation changes, so do the threats. One year in a period of building, plant accidents may be high on the agenda. Another year, as production increases, environmental risks dominate. And in another place, in another country, the threat of kidnap and ransom or extortion may become a problem. As the organisation faces new audiences, problems of safety and security may be an issue.

Having identified the top ten (or more) most likely threats to the

*Figure 2.2* Threat List

Threats will vary a great deal from one organisation to another, but an outline guide is:

| | |
|---|---|
| Accidents | Kidnap/ransom |
| Aircraft accidents | Landslide |
| Allergic reactions | Lawsuits |
| Armed intrusion or hold-up | Lay-offs |
| Bankruptcy/Financial issues | Libel/slander |
| Berserk employee | Lightning |
| Bomb damage | Litigation |
| Boycott | Loss of market |
| Burglary/theft | Loss of shareholder value |
| Business scandal | Malicious damage/vandalism |
| Chemical abuse | Marine accident |
| Chemical spills | Mobile plant accident |
| Civil unrest | Murder |
| Class action | Negative media exposure |
| Collapse of buildings/structures | Oil spill |
| Computer failure | Packaging problems |
| Corporate governance | Personal threats |
| Cyclone | Pollution |
| Damage to reputation | Political problems |
| Death (of customer or employee) | Product failure |
| Demonstrations | Product recall |
| Directors' liability | Product liability |
| Disclosure | Product contamination/tampering |
| Drug abuse | Professional liability |
| Earthquake/Environmental problems | Regulatory changes |
| Ethical crisis | Rumour and innuendo |
| Executive succession or departure | Riots, strikes, civil commotion |
| Explosion | Sabotage |
| Extortion | Sexual harassment |
| Fire | Storm/tempest |
| Government investigation | Sudden market shifts |
| Harbour/port blockage | Suicide |
| Hostile takeover | Suspect mail |
| Infection/disease | Terrorism |
| Information loss/IT Failure | Theft of goods/funds |
| Infrastructure collapse | Whistleblowers |

organisation, the next step is to determine the strategic and tactical responses that would contain and control such an event. Include those audiences, internal and external, with whom the organisation must liaise and to whom it must communicate its actions.

Such response mechanisms should be set by those with immediate responsibility for dealing with them during crisis. They will vary from those threats that are handled first on-site, to those that affect the financial integrity of the organisation and are handled by senior management. Consider how such threats would be dealt with currently, and how your organisation would wish to deal with them given the benefit of foresight.

## GAINING CONSENSUS AND CONTROL

Most organisations have basic plans for protection from various negative events—fire, accidents, water damage, theft, etc. These plans will need to be reviewed in the light of possible escalation to a major disaster or crisis.

Integration with crisis management plans will enable management to maintain control of the corporate agenda in the event of a crisis. For example, do you want the head of a SWAT team, a fire chief, or a corporate watchdog from a government agency speaking publicly on behalf of your company? Very often, many different outside service organisations and government departments can be involved in a crisis response. These groups can dominate your organisation's situation and, if not effectively managed, can become the face of your company, at the same time as dictating the mainstream of messages coming out of the event. It is important to ensure that an organisation's crisis plans incorporate ways and means of dealing with outside support groups working together in the same response.

In response to the TWA Flight 800 that crashed into the sea near Long Island on 17 July 1996, more than 50 disaster and emergency services operations and government agencies came together to initially deal with the disaster, where 230 people lost their lives. At least 20 agencies went on to investigate the accident, deal with the pollution caused on the coastline, counsel friends and relatives, and work towards recovery.

The Mayor of New York became intensely involved in advising next of kin, problems of environmental pollution and getting the message out to the US and international public. The coastguard was involved in underwater salvage of the wreckage and personal belongings. Other Federal officers from a number of agencies participated in the complex range of investigations.

This disaster became a major news item across the United States for months as many families and members of the public believed the handling of the whole situation was a crisis in itself. Many of the post-incident evaluation sessions emphasised the need for greater collaboration between emergency services and government authorities. All these organisations have their separate response plans which eventually need one common planning and communication thread.

Eric Jacoby Jr, Director of the New York State Emergency Management Office, indicated there will be a number of changes in local government crisis management procedures, following the response to the TWA Flight 800 crash. He is working towards a greater linking of disaster and emergency policies for future crisis planning.

Reading the reports from the Contingency Planning Exchange Incorporated, it identified what TWA had to face was far more than an emergency.

It was:

- dealing with distraught families;
- managing an emotional public;
- coping with a huge press response;
- managing rumour and innuendo;
- coping with a large number of government enquiries; and
- management of collecting evidence and finding the cause.

Agendas run high in crises. Political agendas, personal agendas, corporate agendas, emergency agendas, legal agendas. In TWA's case:

- New York's Mayor, Rudolph Guiliani, was concerned about notifying victims' families, the environmental damage and telling the public;
- the coastguard was concerned about recovering evidence from the water and dealing with retrieval of bodies and managing the area of water where the wreckage was located;
- the New York Police Department was concerned about the huge security problems at JFK; in addition to the normal airport traffic, there were literally hundreds of other people making enquiries;
- the FBI was concerned about the Federal and international implications of terrorism; and
- lawyers from around the United States wanted to represent the families and the businesses affected.

There were in fact 21 agencies involved in the investigation, cleaning up the beaches, security of the airport, investigations at the airport, counselling grief-stricken families—21 agencies who were dealing with the crisis management team at TWA. Something like 2000 people. Five hundred media representatives set up operations at the airport and coastguard stations.

The importance of crisis planning and communication was emphasised in all the post-incident evaluations. Planning and communication were *two* areas in which TWA was, quote, 'woefully inadequate' said Mayor Guiliani on US television.

TWA received criticism from many fronts. As a result of the criticism and the Gore Commission for the US Congress, changes have been made to future crisis management strategies.

Some of the problems were:

- TWA was threatened with arrest. They did not release the list of passengers for 24 hours. There were delays in dealing with families still at the airport or those who returned to the airport immediately after the disaster. The press went berserk. Government officials from the City of New York joined family members in their condemnation.

  When TWA's Joanna O'Flaherty arrived to set up a crisis centre at the Ramada Inn, she was threatened with arrest by the New York Police Department for not releasing the passenger list.

- There were too many agencies. During the first few days, the airport and TWA offices were crowded with investigation agencies. The public became very confused about the investigation. At the beginning, there was some dispute over who would be in command. Finally the US President appointed an overall crisis director.

- There was a media invasion of privacy. The *New York Post* obtained a family identification card and invaded the family assistance area. A reporter began to disturb families by soliciting interviews. She was jailed and stripped of her press credentials.

- There was debate about eligibility for family assistance. There were no guidelines as to who should receive assistance. There was no clear definition of who should participate as next of kin— boyfriends, girlfriends, siblings.

- Press briefings did not consider the victims. In the early stages of the disaster, the members of the press were briefed about discoveries *before* members of the families.

- There were problems and issues that arose dealing with communication to families. Problems and issues on the identification and return of bodies, the establishment of a family assistance centre, the return of personal effects, the responsibilities of the air carrier. There was much confusion as to who should deal with this responsibility. The management of briefings and other matters are now the responsibility of the National Transportation Safety Board.
- There was confrontation with lawyers. Litigating attorneys were not allowed into the Emergency Information Centre at the Ramada Inn. This caused a major problem because many of them represented families who were making enquiries at the Centre.

In fact, many lawyers appeared and caused serious problems attempting to push the families into using their law firms with the promise of a lot of money.

- Parents who were estranged fought over the body and the baggage.
- Some passengers had both a spouse and a lover.
- There was poor crisis administration. In terms of crisis administration, no one person had been assigned to arrange faxes, telephones, copying machines and computers with the necessary software programs.
- As 50% of the passengers were of French and Italian nationality it meant that apart from the huge number of US investigation agencies, there were additional government representatives from France and Italy who added to the overall mass investigation. Translation was another problem.
- Rumour was rife. Lack of direction or knowledge can and did result in rumour and innuendo and in this case, it was rife. The media responded to public curiosity about air travel. The crisis was not managed well and the results were, for TWA, devastating.

Most airlines follow a common emergency plan, but like any organisation, interpretation of those plans can be quite different. The way in which threats are identified and responses are performed can be treated quite differently by management teams. The common priority for an airline is that plans are practised and rehearsed with integrated support from emergency services.

In the case of a manufacturing company, it may be necessary to integrate crisis plans with extortion and product recall plans. In the case of an information technology company, it may be necessary to integrate crisis plans with computer failure plans.

The types of plans to be reviewed for integration may include:

- emergency plans;
- computer failure contingency plans;
- contractor emergency plans;
- joint venture partner crisis plans;
- product recall procedures;
- issues management plans;
- environmental management plans;
- evacuation plans;
- kidnap and ransom plans;
- internal or external compliance plans;
- malicious product tampering plans;
- protection plans for executives and employees overseas;
- occupational health and safety plans; and
- security plans.

Consensus is about gaining general agreement among all people concerned in a negative event, so that an escalating crisis is not created by the manner of their public responses. Or where one of the elements in a negative event is not properly identified as a potential crisis. For example:

- A security guard at the gatehouse, dealing with media in an aggressive and confrontational manner. (This results in a lead news story identifying the company and labelling their security methods as hostile and belligerent.)
- A corporate kidnapping is dealt with incompetently by a group of untrained executives. (This can result in an unsatisfactory relationship with the kidnappers and a protracted and highly publicised incident ending in the possible death of the executive involved.)
- A baby food recall that does not sufficiently warn parents of the dangers. (The lack of an early response and effective warning leads to widespread panic and results in the loss of a long-respected brand.)
- An evacuation rehearsal at a 40-storey building causes two heart attacks and an asthma attack amongst evacuees. (The absence of effective research and back-up services in a simple test evacuation results in a number of evacuees being seriously affected by the

drill. This, in turn, results in negative publicity about the safety practices of the organisation.)

* A shipping accident is not reported to head office. (A minor shipping collision results in a major disaster at sea, affecting many lives and losing valuable cargo. The long-term effect is a group insurance investigation and a fall in share price.)

Large organisations may wield great power but can be very quickly brought to their knees by an unexpected event that rapidly takes hold and spreads. It may only be a small incident to start with, but the unintended consequences could have a massive effect on customers, employees, government, suppliers and the competition. If threats are identified and responses prepared, there is a very good chance that the organisation will survive and prosper from the experience.

## EVALUATING PHYSICAL AND TECHNICAL RESOURCES

In 1995 Oklahoma faced one of America's worst acts of urban terrorism when a powerful car bomb ripped into a city building killing hundreds of people. The city's emergency services had to deal with an extraordinary disaster situation. The car bomb turned the city into chaos with bodies lying on footpaths and a huge number of injured people screaming for assistance. It was feared that the nine-storey building itself would collapse and hundreds of people from nearby buildings fled in every direction. It was the ultimate test of every possible emergency services facility, with particular emphasis on panicking relatives looking for their children who were being minded in a day-care centre in the building. The call on additional equipment and resources was enormous.

Long before any crisis event, it is essential to evaluate the additional human and technical facilities that are available. Will there be enough beds in the nearby hospital? Will there be a suitable supplier of blood? Will there be sufficient telephone lines and power? Where will suitable haulage and power cutting equipment be located? Is there sufficient transport and will we need airlift? What about security and counselling? If it is at night, what additional facilities will be required to reduce the chaos?

There is always a need for additional equipment and some of it may be quite sophisticated. In a recent crisis and emergency exercise for a major resource company, consultants identified the need for specific equipment to deal with a major chlorine leak.

The resource location had fire and chemical spill facilities, but chlorine is very corrosive to skin and eyes and contact with the liquid or gas has to be avoided at all costs. Unless protective clothing is worn, serious irritation of the throat, lungs and eyes occurs almost immediately and exposure to a heavy concentration, for even a short period, can be fatal.

Protective clothing has to be worn, but the clothing is more than just a face mask or gloves. Pressurised self-contained breathing apparatus, full face shields, rubber boots as well as gloves and clothing that is impervious to chlorine are all needed. Fully-encapsulating suits may be required in some instances. The exercise identified that the emergency team would have been seriously affected by the escaping chlorine. New equipment and extended training was instigated by the company.

Each office, plant or site will, in most cases, already have an emergency procedure plan in place for control and co-ordination of fires and accidents. As explained previously, these procedures will need to be brought into line with any crisis management and recovery plan. The responsibility of co-ordinating the internal emergency response teams and liaising with the on-site efforts of outside emergency services, such as police, fire brigade and ambulances, is handled by an Emergency Services Co-ordinator, who is a key member of any site crisis management team (see Chapter 3—Creating and Managing a Crisis Team).

A review and examination of the organisation's current emergency procedures to integrate it with crisis planning imperatives will include:

- examining the present emergency response plans to determine their completeness, including site security procedures and external emergency and security assistance required;
- understanding links with contractor and joint venture emergency planning;
- identifying areas to be updated;
- determining the chain of command in roles, responsibilities and authority, in particular, liaison with external emergency services;
- identifying a broad range of resources available on-site and off, including not only emergency services but essential support facilities such as gas, water, electricity, also religious assistance and counselling, interpreter services, and catering; and
- identifying technical assistance required for plant, building and equipment malfunction or accident.

# ASSESSING THE NEEDS OF STAKEHOLDERS

In January 1993, there was a serious food poisoning crisis in the United States where three children died and 144 people were hospitalised after eating hamburgers at a restaurant called 'Jack-in-the-Box'. The restaurant management initially blamed their suppliers, then talked about the serious financial effect the issue would have on the business.

The affected public were left out of the early responses and it was quite a few days before the restaurant management dealt with the issues of the grieving families and concerned customers. A huge number of stakeholders came into play with comments from consumer groups, government and academics. As class actions from victims and share-holders dominated the disaster, the story hit the front pages of newspapers right across the United States and continued for almost a year.

'Jack-in-the-Box' should have understood its stakeholders' needs and may have contained the situation by responding to its audiences rapidly. The whole situation became a crisis in confidence in the restaurant chain.

In every crisis, communication has to start with the first moment in order to maintain effective control. It is an axiom of crisis management, if not business generally, that what you say is as important as what you do, and that you do what you say you will do.

How you deal with the many stakeholders who have an interest, at whatever level, in your organisation, will have a direct bearing on the duration, intensity and economic cost of any crisis. To handle their needs and expectations is no easy task, yet there will be times in a crisis when communication processes are as critical as any physical responses.

Begin with a list of the key stakeholder groups in your organisation. In most organisations, they will be well-defined and well-known audiences, however, during a crisis your stakeholder list will usually include new groups such as investigative media, commentators, academics, investigators and officials.

In a crisis, will your list of stakeholders be enemies or allies? For example, will the local community work with you to solve the problem or work against you and slow up recovery? Will environmentalists come down on you hard if the crisis has a major effect on wildlife? Will shareholders support you because of your financial record or will they turn against you? Without being industry-specific, key stakeholder groups will normally include:

- employees, both those affected and not affected, and next of kin;
- unions;

- senior management and board;
- customers, existing and potential;
- suppliers;
- shareholders;
- financial analysts, bankers;
- insurance companies, legal representatives;
- affected and interested third parties (such as the local community, academics, environmentalists and special interest groups);
- government and its statutory agencies; and
- media and general public.

In a crisis, none of these audiences need be an enemy, but can quickly become one if handled badly. Each audience will need information that is reliable and credible. They will need the facts quickly, and each should receive the same message at the same time. In general, the various stakeholders will want to hear that your organisation, although damaged or threatened by an event or events, is handling the situation in the best possible way, with all due regard to the sensitivity of any human issues.

Above all, they will want to know and understand that you are in control, that any damage, however severe, is minimised and contained, that all injured are being cared for, that the needs of the next of kin of those injured or deceased are being looked after appropriately, and that the organisation is on the road to business recovery. The message strategies for relaying this kind of information are dealt with at length in Chapter 6—Communicating Actions.

The critical factor, however, in controlling the communication process during a crisis, given that a message strategy has been set, is that those within the organisation whose normal corporate responsibility is communicating with each of the stakeholders identified, should continue to do so in a crisis. Speed and accuracy of information is essential.

Thus, for example, corporate treasury or the finance director will communicate with shareholders and financial markets; human resource personnel will have responsibility for unions, employees and next of kin; corporate affairs or corporate communications will handle media; and the CEO will brief the board.

In crisis planning the organisation should ensure that links with each stakeholder group are maintained, so that there is a clear understanding within the company of their information needs, and that in crisis, those needs are fully met.

# CO-ORDINATED OPERATIONAL EVACUATION RESPONSES

Specific crises will require the evacuation of buildings, the immediate area or possibly a whole plant. And do not overlook the fact that an organisation will also be working with a range of external agencies or with a number of separate contractors or shared tenancy teams. Do their plans match your safety practices and your codes of conduct?

Remember, such outside teams can become your frontline partners in the face of a common crisis, and can often inadvertently but quickly damage the message strategy with core stakeholders.

The first responsibility of management will be to move people in immediate danger to safety, while seeing that they are accounted for under existing emergency and evacuation plans. Such plans, however, will need to be brought into line with the crisis management and recovery plan.

To do so, the organisation should consider:

- the types of incidents that might require evacuation;
- the most appropriate mode of evacuation;
- external providers of evacuation resources;
- evacuation communication systems (alarms, telephone, radio, PA system, e-mail);
- individual building and area evacuation plans with muster points;
- safety officers' control;
- distribution and display of plans, including copies held at corporate headquarters;
- accountability for co-ordination;
- emergency lighting and night-time back-up;
- criteria for movement of priority equipment and documents;
- evacuation of key equipment; and
- an evacuation log and up-to-date employee and contractor lists.

The responsibility of co-ordinating the emergency response teams, evacuation wardens and first-aid crews is handled by the Emergency Services and Security Co-ordinator, who is a key member of the crisis management team (see Chapter 3—Creating and Managing a Crisis Team).

# CONTROL POINTS

- ☐ Threats need to be identified at least twice a year.

- ☐ Separate threats from risks.

- ☐ Determine threat impact on assets, earnings, people, environment and reputation.

- ☐ Decide on strategic and tactical responses to control threats.

- ☐ Integrate emergency plans, issues management plans, evacuation plans, product recall plans, security plans and environment plans with crisis plans.

- ☐ Evaluate your resources in light of major threats—can you respond adequately to control?

# 3

# CREATING AND MANAGING
# A CRISIS TEAM

'He's flying British Airways to London and I don't expect to hear from him for hours.' The CEO is uncontactable. The three decision-makers in the company cannot be found. All the senior secretary can do is to keep trying to locate one of the management group. Two television channels and the '60 Minutes' crew have arrived outside the offices wanting answers. Environmentalists have set up camp in the park opposite. The public is calling for answers on talkback radio. The onslaught becomes more aggressive. And this company has not even briefed its lawyers let alone its own executive management team. The search is on to find an executive to manage the crisis. No crisis team, no leader.

---

The first stage of any crisis management and recovery plan is to select a responsible and capable team to manage a crisis. The team should comprise a core group of managers skilled in several critical disciplines. They will be assigned specific responsibilities for before, during and after a crisis, and will be authorised and empowered to make decisions for the entire organisation in times of crisis. The team should be small, so that its members can make decisions quickly.

In this regard, they do not have to be top executives, but they must be trained, capable of taking command and able to activate systems and break through the bureaucracy. Most of all, they need to have clear lines of authority and information. Those appointed to the team must possess an understanding of both internal and external perspectives, have solid negotiating skills, grace under pressure, and the ability to deal effectively with conflict.

Through the crisis management plan, a head office or Crisis Organisational Response Executive (CORE) team, needs to be established with the authority to provide corporate leadership and management of the crisis management plan.

Their role is not just to provide leadership from head office during a crisis, but to direct and provide ongoing training, finance, material and equipment to other teams across the organisation. This permanent group should ensure the development of crisis management procedures and provide a wide variety of support capabilities to site and location teams.

Each site and location should have its own team based on the CORE structure. Organisations that copy their head office team structure at each site and location facilitate a much more free-flowing structure and provide each team with the ability to adapt quickly to a crisis that may develop either at a site or location and move up to head office or at head office moving down through the organisation. There needs to be a total interrelationship of each crisis team's component parts.

By adapting a mutual team structure and agreeing to replicate roles and responsibilities, decision time is reduced and there is increased significance in decisions at each level. Also by having a similar structure of crisis teams across the organisation, team effectiveness is improved as members learn to think in one direction. If a site or location crisis requires assistance from a head office or business unit team, then members of those teams can quickly adapt and think together.

The synergy of team decision-making depends on a similar team structure being in place at each office and location. It should also be said that the leadership of each team, whether it be the CORE group or a location or site team, must be given the authority to act individually and independently in the early stages of any crisis event.

If your organisation was starting from scratch in developing a crisis management team or teams, you could follow the process outlined below.

1. Identify the head office CORE crisis management team and gain managerial commitment to develop a crisis plan and teams across the organisation.
2. Decide on similar teams at each division, plant, location, site and subsidiary.
3. Integrate the plan consistent with the overall organisational policies and procedures.
4. Develop training, testing and maintenance at every level.

# THE CRISIS MANAGEMENT TEAM

We have already established that every crisis is different and will require specific responses. However, the duties and responsibilities of team members do follow a common path. Managing a crisis response is a complex and demanding process—it requires a team of people from both top and middle management. All team members need to have their roles and duties laid out in terms of what to do before the crisis occurs—the preparation stage; what to do when the crisis happens—the response stage; and what to do afterwards—the recovery stage.

Developing a crisis management team in itself is a valuable team-building experience. It gives a group of managers the chance to prepare themselves with strategies appropriate to assist in saving the organisation when it is in trouble. The process contributes both to organisational well-being and the business of the bottom line.

The team should be made up of a team leader who plays an active part in driving the philosophy of the process through the team and across the organisation. The leader is also responsible for the selection, training and review of other team members. This person must be able to cope with pressure and understand the corporate culture as well as setting the standards for developing responses in line with organisational structures. An alternative team leader needs to be identified and trained alongside the leader—in the case of an extended crisis running over a number of days, the alternative team leader will provide a critical support factor.

The emergency services and security team member has a wide-ranging role which essentially ensures that internal and external emergency response actions are in place and that any additional support or logistical assistance is provided. This role provides the essential link with police, fire, ambulance and rescue. It may well involve contact with state or national disaster organisations. This role also co-ordinates security requirements so that the organisation and the crisis team can operate in a safe and secure environment.

The team member who is responsible for getting the message out has the corporate affairs and media responsibility. This is a role of both co-ordination and provision of messages. Not only does the corporate affairs and media co-ordinator have to liaise with the major audiences affected by a crisis, but they have to design and distribute messages at each phase of the event. Their role before the crisis happens is about setting up links between communities, customers, government, media and so on.

Employees need to know what has happened. The human resources and family co-ordinator's role is initially to advise employees what has happened and what their part is in either the control of the crisis or the recovery from the crisis. At the same time, this role involves dealing with victims' families and the sensitive issues related to advice on death and injury. The human resources co-ordinator also needs to be responsible for letting employees know how the crisis management plan works within the organisation and how it assists them in times of serious emergencies.

The administration role will provide and co-ordinate all the essential business services required by the crisis management team. It is not necessary to have a room full of administration managers, lawyers, accountants and insurance advisers during a crisis. This role ensures that the skills base of experts is effectively briefed and can provide advice as required.

An operational manager needs to be available for the crisis team. Whether the problem is a major accident shutting down part of a plant, whether it be a major product recall where products have to be withdrawn from supermarkets and warehouses, or whether it is an ethical issue related to the way business is done, the event will require operational advice and action. This team member needs to have a mature and complete understanding of the cause and effect of a crisis on the production process and be prepared to present the broadest range of problems and opportunities to the team leader.

In all organisations, business continuity is essential when a crisis hits. The role of business continuity and recovery plays an important part in the process. No matter what threat is being dealt with by the team, the business must continue and be returned to normality as soon as possible. This co-ordinator needs to make on-the-spot decisions which ensure stability of the business and recovery of plant and operations as soon as possible. He or she needs to have a clear understanding of all facets of the organisation as much of the work will be done prior to any crisis event where upon establishing the threats and risks to the organisation, recovery goals for assets and earnings will be identified.

The role of calling out the team and running the actual technology of a control room is a function often overlooked. It is all very well having a crisis team and a crisis plan, but someone has to be responsible for getting the team together and providing a suitable location, with facilities, to meet in. This control room and call-out co-ordinator establishes immediate contact with the team and sets up the necessary equipment to allow them to operate efficiently.

# TEAM FUNCTIONS, DUTIES AND TASKS CHECKLISTS

## Team leader

*Function*

Responsible for: confirming the crisis status, co-ordinating the team, liaising with board and CEO, allocating resources, setting priorities and selecting and briefing the spokesperson.

*Duties and tasks*

*Before*

- [ ] Confirm crisis plan and gain CEO and managerial approval
- [ ] Identify crisis team members
- [ ] Assign roles and responsibilities
- [ ] Ensure links to all divisions, subsidiaries and affiliates
- [ ] Arrange training, testing and maintenance of plan

*During*

- [ ] Confirm the problem
- [ ] Brief team members on situation
- [ ] Action response measures and delegate tasks
- [ ] Set up logging process
- [ ] Continually confirm and search out information
- [ ] Brief CEO, directors and board
- [ ] Call in additional skills where needed
- [ ] Advise alternative leaders
- [ ] Regularly update team

*After*

- [ ] Provide response overview and debrief
- [ ] Provide evaluation of plans and procedures
- [ ] Revise plans accordingly
- [ ] Review equipment and facilities

## Corporate affairs and media

*Function*

Responsible for: messages for stakeholders, media management, spokesperson briefing, business/financial issues and feedback from internal and external sources to the team.

## Duties and tasks
*Before*
- [ ] Identify key audiences
- [ ] Agree on spokesperson
- [ ] Encourage procedures for message and information distribution at all levels of the organisation
- [ ] Set up media contact networks
- [ ] Confirm approval procedure for information release with senior management and legal
- [ ] Agree to location for media conference or briefing
- [ ] Arrange media training

*During*
- [ ] Focus on confirmation of facts
- [ ] Prepare initial messages, gain approval and release
- [ ] Brief spokesperson
- [ ] Co-ordinate internal and external messages
- [ ] Liaise with legal and risk management
- [ ] Monitor media
- [ ] Provide background information
- [ ] Consider web site information update
- [ ] Co-ordinate media briefings and conferences

*After*
- [ ] Review communication strategies
- [ ] Provide post-briefing strategy for key audiences
- [ ] Review all media coverage and editorials
- [ ] Debrief support staff

## Human resources and family

*Function*
Responsible for: welfare, rehabilitation, counselling, and communication of news to employees and victims' families.

## Duties and tasks
*Before*
- [ ] Establish status of employee contact capability
- [ ] Inform employees of organisational policy on crisis management
- [ ] Set up support skills base for medical, counselling, welfare, etc.
- [ ] Identify communication guidelines to advise employees on situation

*During*
- [ ] Confirm status of event and effect on personnel

☐ Prepare and distribute information for employees on status of operations

☐ Initiate victims' information and provide support services

☐ Contact victims' families

☐ Provide information hot lines and e-mail news update

☐ Brief legal counsel

*After*

☐ Continue to monitor victims' assistance and support

☐ Provide ongoing information and advice to employees on status of organisation

☐ Review human resources capabilities during crisis

## Emergency and security

*Function*

Responsible for: emergency services, site and personnel security, external assistance, and evacuation.

*Duties and tasks*

*Before*

☐ Establish status of all internal emergency services and security facilities

☐ Arrange co-ordinated rehearsals between crisis team and emergency support teams

☐ Confirm call-out procedures for outside emergency services—police, ambulance, fire

☐ Identify additional support requirements—security, airlift, evacuation, transport

*During*

☐ Confirm emergency response actions and status of incident

☐ Ensure safety of emergency teams

☐ Alert external emergency services and call for assistance, if necessary

☐ Provide additional support for security of assets and personnel

☐ Continually identify status of incident and effect on operations

☐ Maintain communications with emergency control centre

*After*

☐ Debrief and review interaction with emergency management and response

☐ Review logs and support from internal and external emergency services

☐ Determine effectiveness of emergency response

☐ Review crisis management plans and advise team leader on problems and opportunities related to interaction

☐ Debrief outside emergency services and ask for evaluation of internal response

## Operations

*Function*

Responsible for: management of local and international operations, liaising with crisis team on operational issues, and links with marketing and distribution.

*Duties and tasks*

*Before*

☐ Identify and measure threats relative to operations and effects on customers

☐ Identify triggers for crisis from operational accidents, issues, product recall, bad weather, and so on

☐ Confirm alternative means of operations

*During*

☐ Focus on operation and business continuity

☐ Organise alternative means of supply/production

☐ Confirm implementation of product recall, if necessary

☐ Anticipate effects on major customers and advise sales and marketing departments

☐ Execute plans to provide outside support for maintenance of operations

*After*

☐ Report on status of operations

☐ Review adequacy of operations and adjust

☐ Review crisis plan related to operational problems

☐ Review threat analysis and advise team

## Command centre and call-out

*Function*

Responsible for: alert and call-out of team, command centre set-up, communication equipment, communications operations, logging of the incident, support staff, emergency switchboard operators and catering.

*Duties and tasks*

*Before*

☐ Responsible for being alerted about all serious incidents that may escalate to crisis

☐ Assesses the level of incident by prior arrangement and initiates notification of crisis team

☐ Arranges the set up and facilities of crisis control room

☐ Initiates all necessary support staff for control room

☐ Initiates procedures review and tests regularly

☐ Organises and confirms 24-hour capability

*During*

☐ Calls out crisis team

☐ Ensures control room is equipped and operational

☐ Maintains and executes logging procedures

☐ Obtains additional whiteboards and cellular telephones

☐ Controls access to room

☐ Provides catering facilities

☐ Maintains a register of calls

☐ Assists with the set up of additional facilities such as video conference, media conference room and special room for CEO brief

*After*

☐ Debrief support group

☐ Provide team leader with review of systems and facilities

☐ Replenish and renew any used or out-of-date equipment

## Administration

*Function*

Responsible for: legal, insurance and financial issues.

*Duties and tasks*

*Before*

☐ Verify organisational legal, insurance and accounting requirements for crisis status

☐ Confirm support roles for legal, risk/insurance and financial

☐ Confirm arrangements with contractors, suppliers and consultants under crisis status

*During*

☐ Advise crisis team on legal and risk issues related to employees, assets, environment and third party

☐ Co-ordinate legal counsel to provide essential information for crisis team leader and other team members

- [ ] Provide legal support for public announcements
- [ ] Review procedures for handling third party claims
- [ ] Confirm legal obligations for employees, authorities and other third parties
- [ ] Co-ordinate risk management and insurance advice
- [ ] Provide link with treasury on financial support and assistance
- [ ] Authorise and organise appropriate internal management and staff assistance or outside consultant support

*After*

- [ ] Instigate internal audit and investigation into crisis management response
- [ ] Review support from all commercial services
- [ ] Debrief outside consultants
- [ ] Provide budget and cost for crisis response and recovery

## Recovery

*Function*

Responsible for: identifying recovery strategies, identifying resources and managing the business resumption.

*Duties and tasks*

*Before*

- [ ] Evaluate threats and establish recovery and business resumption objectives for each threat
- [ ] Establish process for recovery with managerial agreement
- [ ] Confirm with Operations team member how contingency plans would work

*During*

- [ ] Co-ordinate with Human resources and family team member on issues related to employees and victims
- [ ] Immediately ensure business continuity
- [ ] Work with Operations co-ordinator to begin recovery of assets and earning
- [ ] Advise team on recovery stream of actions

*After*

- [ ] Review recovery issues related to employees and victims
- [ ] Continue recovery strategies related to assets and earnings
- [ ] Review recovery issues related to effects on customers, community, shareholders

Depending on the organisation, its size and complexity, the final make-up of the team will be tailored to suit (see Figure 3.1). For example, a financial institution may well have a key role for specialists from its treasury, a resource company might add an environmental role, and a food company a quality assurance or product recall role.

Reporting to the crisis management team will normally also be a support group, made up of specialist areas of expertise, such as technical operations, management information systems, legal, secretarial, government liaison, and facilities management.

Relative to the organisational structure or spread, there may be a need for several such teams, each with similar make-up. For example, a crisis management team at individual sites, a team for business units or for international regions, and a corporate team at head office. And while any crisis is best handled on-site by local teams, an escalating crisis will involve the full resources of the organisation, with trigger points for control or strategic advice between each level of command.

Similarly, because many executives are off-site or overseas at any given moment, each crisis management team, at whatever level, must have nominated alternates who can take over the designated roles of those who are absent.

## LEADERSHIP FROM THE TOP— CEO COMMITMENT

There is no hiding place in a crisis, particularly when dealing with the media. And when the 'big one' hits, it is the CEO who ends up facing

*Figure 3.1* Crisis management team

the music. But, while the CEO is a cultural figurehead in any crisis, he or she may not necessarily be the one that acts as the leading spokesperson. The CEO role is one of calm and decisive leadership.

Even if the CEO is flying high, locked in political combat with a president or even resting reclusively on a desert island, it is essential that he or she is involved. In so many of the most highly publicised crises, especially where corporate inaction is criticised, it is inevitably the CEO who is pursued for their views and opinions. What did the CEO do? What did he or she say? Could the CEO perform under pressure? The commitment to a fast, effective recovery needs to come from the CEO. Every stakeholder involved in the organisation knows that the company stands the best chance of surviving if the leadership is strong and the commitment has no barriers.

When the horrific accident occurred at Bhopal in India in 1984 and poisonous gas spread over 25 square miles killing thousands of people, Union Carbide's Chief Executive acted fast. Warren Anderson went straight to Bhopal and made himself available to the government, the media, the employees' families and the community.

He faced the music and was besieged with inquiries. But as he dealt with one of the worst crises in modern history, he knew that control could only be conveyed by leadership from the top. He became the very face of Union Carbide on the spot. Anderson repeated the story in detail and kept the media updated on developments. He was candid and credible and in control of the message agenda. He could have run for cover and delegated the responsibility to a number of other people.

The public needed to hear from the top as to why the *Exxon Valdez* oil spill occurred at Prince William Sound in 1989. The CEO was not available. Exxon was very slow to react and moved the blame away from the company. Overall, their spokespeople were unprepared and initially uncontactable. As a result of top management's absence, the agenda was highjacked by the media, the community, the government and many stakeholders. The public saw a disaster beginning to take shape and no clear leadership appeared in sight.

In 1997 in Australia, the Managing Director of Arnott's Biscuits, Chris Roberts, knew there was no hiding place when he headed up the crisis management team that dealt with the extortion attempt against the company. He knew that taking leadership was taking control. He understood that controlling the agenda was the beginning of a solid recovery for his company and for its brands. His active endorsement played a major role in drawing the rest of the organisation into supporting their crisis management plan.

In another Australian incident involving Kraft brand products, their Managing Director, Tom Park, opted for the slower strategy. It took him some days to appear as the face of Kraft's peanut butter contamination crisis. While Kraft's brand came under siege, we watched the Company Secretary cope with intense media scrutiny and criticism. Tom Park made a fairly relaxed appearance later in the week and began to manage the crisis with a determination to protect the image of the company and its wide range of valuable products. This crisis in brand confidence severely affected their top selling brand, which is still recovering.

For companies to maximise their potential for dealing with crisis, the superior approach is to ensure management has strategically positioned the company to cope. This, in turn, hinges on the management culture of the company, and on the commitment of the CEO to crisis preparedness. Most crises, and, indeed, the majority of reasons for business failure, are not directly technological or financial problems, but rather the result of organisational, social, political and communication issues. For the most part, such crises can also be foreseen, if only conceptually.

Ensuring the cultural approach to crises is a positive one is the task of a CEO. The ultimate responsibility in crisis will lie with the CEO. It is the CEO who must live with crisis, expect it and be prepared for it, and who must plan strategically for crisis as a normal part of business operations. It is the CEO who must oversee an organisational and management culture and structure that can cope with crisis, and who should understand best the cause and effect of crisis on the organisation. And yet, the levels of unreadiness, inexperience and defensive reactions that still exist within many an organisation generally indicate that the lessons have not yet been learnt. There is really no excuse for the CEO who does not comprehend the many common characteristics that exist between business problems and crises.

On the other hand, there is no single management style that is best suited to crisis management. The most successful, however, will be one that recognises the possibility of crisis, identifies the threats and issues ahead of time as part of ongoing best practice management, and ensures the organisation is able to respond actively and positively to crisis so that control is maintained at all times over the corporate destiny. Therefore, taking a lead at the crisis planning stage is one of the most valuable business activities of the modern CEO. The commitment shown to crisis preparedness will cascade through the organisation, and ensure the company has appropriate responses at all levels and at every stage in a crisis.

Equally, the CEO can often have a specific role in leading the crisis management team, transferring business skills directly to the resolution of the event and the protection of assets, earnings, personnel and the environment. The strategic focus of the CEO is then a valuable tool in giving direction to those most immediately involved in handling the event.

## CEO ACTION LIST

What does the CEO need to consider in the face of a major crisis?

- The primary role is to provide corporate direction on resolving the problem and to minimise the impact on employees, the corporate reputation, the community and share value.
- Immediately, it is important to confirm the real situation. Getting accurate facts is sometimes difficult when the pressure is mounting, however, analysing the facts in order to identify response actions has to be a key objective in the early stages.
- Two streams of action are needed. One stream to manage the crisis response and one stream to manage the daily business. Life goes on, and although a crisis can stop an organisation in its tracks, business resumption is essential and part of the immediate recovery process.
- Take into consideration at all times the corporate position. Confirm a consistent message strategy and make sure that one spokesperson is giving a clear message right across all stakeholder audiences.
- Confirm how the crisis is affecting the company's audiences. Research can be very important here, and employing research to monitor attitudes to the response can be invaluable on the road to recovery.
- Be prepared to lose business and market share initially to gain maximum results in your response. (Johnson & Johnson withdrew the Tylenol product in the United States after the extortion poisoning, initially losing market share. They repackaged in tamper-proof packs under government supervision and quickly regained brand reputation and market share.)
- Take the initiative. Be prepared to tell it as it is. Show the stakeholders what you are doing and why you are doing it. Emphasise and use language the community understands. Clarify information rather than promise results.
- Do not let lawyers slow down the crisis agenda. Take good legal advice but avoid being gagged on disclosure.

- Importantly, do not lose control of yourself or your temper. Overreaction can cause confusion in the response process and a lack of confidence in the company. There will be dramatic changes in information and they have to be dealt with responsibly.
- Keep a close eye on your competitors. They will use your crisis time as an opportunity.
- Get on top of your financial audience before they are led by business analysts, academics and financial journalists. Help the financial analysts, the banks and your insurers understand that you are on top of the issues and controlling market vulnerabilities.
- Enlist industry and government support. Make sure your industry and the government understand the seriousness of your problem and do all they can to support your recovery.
- Most of all, think ahead. Use lateral thinking to interpret both unintended consequences and how the business may finish up. Direct your recovery team to start building bridges and repairing reputation now.

If the event is long and drawn out, be sure to get rest and keep stress at bay. During the Second World War, Winston Churchill used to take constant naps at the peak of his performance in the war room deep beneath London. Leadership can only be achieved if a leader is prepared to keep a flexible and rested mind.

Having a single-minded sense of purpose signals an organisation that is ready to deal with the worst. A leader who is committed and focused on a planned crisis response will bring positive results and successful business resumption ... without any need to find a hiding place.

## COMMAND AND CONTROL— THE MODERN WAR ROOM

One of the immediate requirements during a crisis will be the establishment of a crisis command centre. This is where the crisis management team fulfil their specific roles designed to contain and manage the crisis. This command centre should not be confused with an emergency services communications centre, where emergency teams receive their commands and directions.

This command centre is the management centre for crisis response and information. It operates as a focal point for reporting the crisis status. It is where the crisis team administers the crisis response and issues instructions to those directly concerned at the crisis location.

Planning should include a number of alternative command centre locations. In case the selected room is not available or is rendered inoperable because of an accident, the team should have one or two off-site options. It is wise to have a second command centre location at a branch office or joint venture office nearby. Many organisations share crisis management resources with similar businesses and therefore the command centre could be located in another organisation's command room set up.

A crisis control centre will require:

- a central location;
- suitable construction;
- fire and storm protection;
- reliable security;
- communications equipment, such as secure telephone lines, modems to access data bases, facsimile machines, satellite television capability, video-conferencing facilities, internal directories, maps and site drawings, crisis manuals, safety equipment, radio links, whiteboards, incident and call logs, catering facilities; and
- an adjoining quiet area for the team leader to confer.

The command centre needs to be accessible any time of the day or night (see Figure 3.2). It should be able to swing into action in a matter of minutes. If a boardroom or meeting room takes an hour to set up, then it will hold the crisis team up in their decision-making actions.

A team member should be appointed to maintain the command centre at operational readiness. Telephone lines, facsimile lines and any special facilities should be installed well-ahead and tested in a number of practice runs.

There should also be a command centre travel case (i.e. ready to go to any crisis site). This should contain checklists, crisis management response (CMR) manual, satellite telephones, cellular telephone, laptop computer, two-way radio, audio-recorder, camera and torches. It should also contain cash, credit cards, batteries and blank ID cards.

In choosing the right position of the room, the team should consider the security aspects of the facility and make sure that it is well away from the foyer or any other public areas. The team does not want to be moving in and around the media and other stakeholders during the pressure of the event.

A crisis has no set time. Some protracted events last for days and even weeks. The room needs to be spacious and capable of dealing with people movement. At the same time, it needs to have access to

*Figure 3.2* The crisis command centre

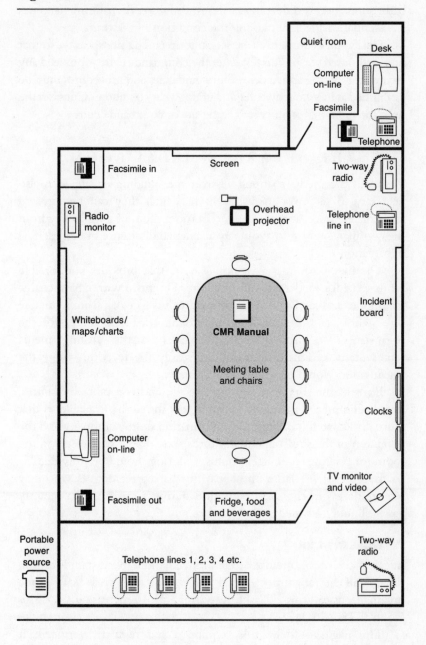

the organisation's facilities and systems. It also needs access to bathrooms and even sleeping facilities. Provision for catering becomes an essential part of maintaining the condition of the team.

Finally, procedures must be set up for retaining site security, so that non-authorised persons do not enter the command centre, or indeed any secure area, during an incident. Entry guidelines and procedures must be established as to who may enter and under what conditions. Consider the need for additional security staff at the site or command centre.

## THE SEPARATE MEDIA ROOM

To avoid the media roaming all over the building or site, it is also necessary to set up a media room to which they can be directed immediately upon arrival. The media room should be well away from the command centre to avoid any accidental disclosure of confidential information.

The media room is a working centre that provides comfortable work space for media attending the site. Equipped with tables, chairs, telephones and facsimiles, it allows journalists to work from a suitable base station, at the same time as providing a briefing area for the organisation to present regular updates to the visiting media representatives. This area is not necessarily the location where the organisation would present a press conference.

Plans of the site, with appropriate site and corporate brochures, fact sheets and the media information kit, should be available so that journalists have full background information on the company and the operation of the site concerned. Media should be asked to stay in the room for briefings on current status. Catering should be provided.

Because of the large number of media representatives who may require access to the site or location during a crisis, media security passes should be issued.

### Portable crisis kit

In case a crisis team member has to move rapidly to a distant location, there will be an urgent need for a portable crisis kit. Some organisations call this a 'Taskforce Crisis Kit'. In my case it's a 'Crisis Control Travel Bag'.

This bag should be fully equipped and regularly serviced. It contains all the necessary accoutrements that a crisis manager might need 'on the road'. Here is the ideal crisis tool for crisis managers involved in the transport industry or exploration business.

This 'Crisis Control Travel Bag' contains crisis action checklists, mobile phone and/or iridium satellite phone, Global Position Satellite Receiver, laptop computer, high-powered torch, batteries, radio, tape-recorder, camera, film, pager, medical kit, contacts lists, stationery, money, credit cards, passports and ID.

---

## CONTROL POINTS

☐ Crisis needs a team response from a trained group of managers.

☐ Alternatives are vital for every team member.

☐ The main team should be represented by key skills in line with corporate structure.

☐ The team roles should be replicated through all divisions, units, sites and locations.

☐ A support group will be needed to provide specialist expertise and secretarial services.

☐ The CEO should be a cultural figurehead in every crisis plan.

☐ The buck stops with the CEO. In a rapid escalation, the sooner the CEO leads the agenda, the better.

☐ A crisis command centre is needed for each team, equipped with the necessary technical facilities.

☐ A room for the media should be identified.

---

# 4

# THE INTERNAL AUDIENCE

They were a close family and they had waited patiently by the telephone since they heard the news of the accident at the mine site on the radio. Still no news of their son. He was on the dusk shift and would have been underground when the shaft collapsed, bringing down tons of rock on the small team of miners. Then they heard his name—'Ernst'. One of the foremen who came up was being interviewed by the local radio station and he reeled off the names of the men who were hit by the fall. This is the first they knew about Ernst being a victim. Nobody had called from the company. Nobody had told the family that Ernst might be in trouble. Nobody made the call.

Employees and families must be told of a crisis first and fast. Effective crisis planning requires managers to report on the importance of the situation to every level of the organisation quickly and efficiently. Rumour and innuendo need to be controlled with the same efficiency that an emergency crew uses to deal with a fire. And it means a level of communication that many managers may not have applied before. Sensitivity and strength of message will produce positive results.

The 'Tell 'em nothing' or 'we'll let them know later' approach is a certain recipe for disaster. Losing this valuable audience in the first few hours of a crisis greatly devalues the message strategy to all stakeholders.

Addressing employee issues first will enlist an army of support. In the case of a company that is going through a major product recall or dealing with a serious accident in the workplace, the first people the media will seek out for information are employees. If employees have a clear idea of what has happened, then facts lead the story instead of scandal and hearsay.

Employees form their own opinions quickly. Will the crisis destroy the organisation and will they have a job? Is the company responsible? Having a plan of action in place to address employees' concerns enables a company to move the message to its other stakeholders with the confidence that the whole organisation understands the situation. It also assists in the recovery and business resumption process because employees are more willing to return to a normal work environment. Also, if people are better informed, they are considerably more willing to assist in getting the company back on track again.

For example, in a 1996 crisis faced by Hitachi at Greenville, South Carolina, a truck careered off an interstate highway into a restaurant, killing three and injuring two Hitachi employees, all Japanese citizens working temporarily in the United States. Hitachi's communication with the next of kin was efficient and planned as was their communication with employees.

As Caroline Bobo wrote in the *Public Relations Quarterly* of the incident on 18 July, 1996:

"The company's response to families' needs made a statement about Hitachi Electronic Devices USA (HED US) philosophy to all employees. The company's response to the media further supported its concern for survivors of the tragedy, including workmates of the deceased.

" 'I got a call about 8.15 pm telling me there had been an accident at Oyaji', recalled Lawrence W. Davis Jr., Hitachi Vice President for Personnel and Administration. Davis knew that the restaurant was a popular hang-out for employees of Hitachi and other Japanese firms in the area. At the accident scene, Hitachi Vice President Noboru Toyama was on hand to help but could only wait anxiously while officials used a crane to sort through the destruction to extract the deceased men.

"Toyama used Hitachi name badges, the only pictures readily available, to identify the victims at the accident site and at the morgue. Davis arranged for Japanese translators to be at the hospital around the clock to assist the two survivors.

"Hitachi's next step was to deal with the emotional aftershock, the media, Greenville employees, and the victims' families in Japan. Hitachi management established a war room, a plant conference room with chart-covered walls detailing lists of duties, names of family members and others scheduled to arrive from Tokyo or other Hitachi facilities.

" 'We decided to bring everyone in the families, anyone who wanted to come, to Greenville,' said Davis. Many of the victims' family members did not have passports and because of full flights bringing travellers to the nearby Olympic games, available seats on commercial flights were hard to find. However, Hitachi officials at the company's Tokyo headquarters assumed responsibility for travel, passports and the sad task of family notification. (Hitachi's plans to assist the families were of major public interest in Japan, where the families of the deceased were expected to be the company's first concern.) Greenville officials found 30 hotel rooms for family members and arranged for translators to meet families at the airport, accompany them to hotels and assist with arrival and check-in logistics.

"Word of the accident circulated through the Hitachi plant, which operates four shifts. Greenville HED (US) President, Kenichi Fukuzawa prepared a statement that was posted on bulletin boards throughout the plant by 2 am, six hours after the accident. 'We made a decision that we would be frank with everyone, including the media, so long as the families agreed,' said Davis.

"Flags at the plant—United States, South Carolina, and the Hitachi corporate flag—were lowered to half-mast and a flower wreath was placed on the main entrance door, symbols were visible to employees and visitors.

"No shifts were shortened or halted, but supervisors were encouraged to discuss the accident, bereavement and to ask and answer questions.

"Questions were more likely to come from outside the plant, interrupting the multiple tasks associated with the aftermath of unexpected, public death.

"While Davis juggled arrangements, Robert E. Scott, Senior Manager for Personnel and Administration, and Thomas E. Smith, Superintendent of Administration, turned their attention to two high priority issues: a commemorative event and proper cross-cultural planning. Hitachi did not want an unfortunate breach of Japanese etiquette to inflict additional emotional pain on the families.

"Following Japanese tradition, flowers were presented to family members upon arrival, so each could place them at the accident site. A day-long trip was planned so the group could see how their loved ones lived, where they worked and where they died. The family group also travelled to the men's favourite fishing spot and golf course, toured the Hitachi plant and collected personal items—intentionally left untouched by Hitachi and law enforcement officials—from the men's hotel rooms, their homes while living in Greenville. A meeting was also arranged with county solicitors, office attorneys and highway patrol officials to discuss the accident investigation.

"Internal communication included bulletin board notices, a standard Hitachi tactic, and access to information for any department manager or employee. 'We told our employees exactly what was happening, good, bad and indifferent,' said Davis. 'We'd have done the same thing if this had happened in the plant, if a piece of machinery had fallen on people. We wouldn't try to hide anything. The more you try to hide, the worse things get. Employees in need of information may ask their supervisor or security officials, or they can go anywhere in the plant and ask questions', explained Davis.

"Hitachi's Scott requested, through the media, that anyone wishing to express condolences send cards and letters rather than flowers. More than 700 notes were received (two personally delivered by chief executives) and presented to the families at the plant. Local mass media sent reporters to a commemorative tree planting ceremony on the facility campus that was open to all Hitachi employees.

"South Carolina and Buddhist traditions crossed paths at the mortuary. Cremation, preferred by Buddhists, was not possible, because of the length of time between death and the bodies' arrival in Japan. But another Buddhist custom, the placement of photos of the deceased with the remains, was easily accommodated. Enlarged, framed prints of the men's passport photos were placed on closed caskets and given to family members after the visitation. More than 300 people visited the families at the mortuary.

"Early Wednesday morning, July 24, the family entourage—and its three caskets—left Greenville. The two injured men remained hospitalised, then later returned to Japan for additional treatment; one may never walk normally. Local media moved on to other stories, other news. The charts came down from the walls. HED (US) officials made plans for construction related to a plant expansion.

"The rush to help and the immediacy of the event were gone, but there was one lingering issue: there was no acceptance of responsibility from the truck driver. In Japan, people take responsibility for their actions, explained Scott. Had the accident occurred in Japan, the driver would have been expected to visit the families, bring them gifts, visit the injured in hospital and express his remorse and sorrow. 'The families couldn't understand why he wasn't there, or wasn't willing to take responsibility', noted Scott. The accident was a front-page newspaper story in Japan, with concern focused on the well-being of the families and the acceptance of responsibility by the driver or his employer. Greenville Hitachi officials have power of attorney for the families; litigation continues."

# MANAGEMENT RESPONSIBILITY TO EMPLOYEES

Management, therefore, has a two-fold responsibility in crisis planning for its employees. First of all, set up clear lines of communication to effectively reach them in the workplace and/or at home and give them the message. Second, establish a procedure on how to deal with employee problems related to the event.

In many post-evaluations of crisis incidents, employee issues dominate the recovery effort. Where employees go to get information needs to be pre-determined. Do they continue to report to the same manager for day-to-day news or are there dedicated telephone lines, meeting rooms and discussion points? Has the organisation developed a monitoring system for post-traumatic stress and what ongoing back-up services are available for families of victims? Are there funds available to support victims of a company crisis and are these funds accessible quickly?

Does local and international transport need to be provided to bring in support for families at distant operations? If certain businesses have to be closed down, how will lay-offs or job replacement be handled?

Seriously injured employees often come under intense media focus in an escalating crisis. It is the human issues, the emotional factors and the sensitive relationships with their families that naturally dominate the front-page news.

Long before the news cameras arrive at the plant site or the victim's family home, the message of what has happened should have reached the family and most employees. Those who witnessed the event and those involved in any rescue should have been counselled. Minimising trauma across the immediate scene will damp down panic and assist the organisation's ongoing recovery strategy.

## UPDATING THE FACTS

Talking to employees is not a one-off communication during a crisis. Planning must include ways of continually updating and upgrading information. They will need to know about the emergency response and about the direction the organisation is taking. Essentially, for every message to the media, there should be a prior message to employees.

Depending on the nature of the event, this can be done through one-to-one briefings by managers and foremen, large group meetings in a public building, hot lines or organised telephone messages to homes, briefings at evacuation areas, copies of information being handed out at the gate or entrance, public address announcements, using the local media such as radio and even e-mail or the Internet.

Clear guidelines need to be established well in advance for notifying families in the case of any fatality or injury. The tyranny of time faces management because of the need to reach loved ones before the event is made public. Needless to say, all information regarding names, injuries or cause of death must be withheld until authorised. The authorisation process is an integral part of emergency planning, particularly at isolated sites, plants or locations.

If lessons have been learned from Australia's tragic mining accidents over the last few years, clear steps will be taken to fast track family records and information in cases of serious accidents. The speed and care with which a company deals with a family's concern and well-being can mitigate against public backlash. Importantly, the employee's family is more likely to care about the company when the company puts itself out for the employee's family.

The other issue that must be dealt with rapidly is compensation. While there may be a barrage of legal and financial reasons why this cannot happen quickly, organisations have to set up systems to minimise delays. Next of kin need to be cared for urgently and their recovery monitored continually. The company's top management needs to see that compensation is being prioritised.

## PREPARATION FOR EMPLOYEE COMMUNICATION

Effective ways of telling employees about crisis preparedness must come long before a crisis happens. Crisis planning should incorporate an employee policy statement that includes reference to the company's commitment in controlling crises, contingency plans for the company's people and links with occupational health and safety standards. The statement should state that the crisis management plan is designed to minimise risks to employees and to the community. It also should point out the clear channels of communication that are available for information flow during a crisis.

A common reason for barriers to the communication of bad news is the relationship between a company and its contractors. Because different systems are used by the company and the contractor, critical delays can occur in the procedure. Pre-crisis planning must take into consideration the co-ordination of company plans with contractor plans. By integrating essential contact methodology, crisis managers will have more control over reaching families urgently.

Any crisis planning process is as much a people-saving strategy as a face-saving strategy. It is therefore essential that the human resources and family co-ordinator on the crisis management team deals with concerns and threats facing employees in the pre-crisis planning stage rather than attempting to sort out the problems during an actual crisis.

To be effective, this planning must be part of the overall strategy and incorporated into a procedures manual for the purpose.

Ahead of any major emergency or crisis, a number of essential tactics will prepare the organisation to deal with employee and next of kin issues (these can be dealt with by the human resources and family co-ordinator in the crisis management team):

- designate who is accountable for co-ordinating communications with employees and next of kin;
- arrange training for company personnel and other supporting counsellors or advisers who may be called upon to deliver bad news to next of kin;
- make provisions for an office to be established to manage enquiries from employees and next of kin;
- establish a record of all employees' next of kin, with full contact details;
- establish clear guidelines on communication with contractors, consultants and temporary employees;
- arrange protection of families from the media;
- develop a message strategy with the spokesperson and a continual drip-feed of information for distribution or delivery to employees and next of kin; and
- establish effective communications so that all employee groups gain information about the status of the incident simultaneously.

In a crisis, there are a number of essential employee and next of kin communication responsibilities:

- account for all employees, and give them a briefing on the status of the event;
- communicate the ongoing situation to employees on a regular basis, without dramatising it;
- be prepared to listen to their comments and grievances;
- provide communications facilities for them to contact their families; and
- ensure that counselling, interpreter and transport services are available for those who require them.

Finally, as a number of company employees can play a major role in the recovery process after any crisis, the following should also be addressed:

- be prepared to debrief employees;
- commence briefing as soon as possible on their job status;

- communicate their part in the recovery plan; and
- continue to drive and monitor the welfare and support program.

## MANAGING THE BAD NEWS, COUNSELLING AND NEXT OF KIN

This is a highly sensitive communication area, and should be handled by company executives where company personnel are involved. Certainly there are trained counsellors, usually with a psychology degree, who understand exactly how to approach the sensitive problem of communicating bad news. This tragic and sensitive job is often handed to a young police officer who is usually ill-experienced and ill-prepared to present the bad news to a family. Neither is the police officer prepared to cope with what might follow in terms of a serious emotional response, physical collapse or, at worst, an asthma or heart attack.

There is a lesson to be learned from a woman in a distant West Australian mining town who tells the story about a policeman waking her from a deep sleep in the early hours of the morning. Upon opening the door and recognising the local officer, he presented the news to the half-awake recipient: 'Sorry to tell you that your daughter's been killed in a road smash near the town and I've got to get back there fast'.

The policeman had his job to do and could not be in two places at once so he left the highly distressed and shocked woman to deal with this tragedy on her own, alone. She waited for the morning to come, and after pulling herself together, walked through the local supermarket looking for some contact with the people of the town. The few people in the supermarket avoided her with deliberation. They had heard about the story but did not have the ability or the strength of mind to face this woman. It was not until later that day that real help arrived on her doorstep—some of the wives of the mining community got together and gave her the support that should have come hours before.

The delivery of bad news should not be left to emergency services personnel, or, even worse, by way of news broadcasts. Training or briefing on the techniques should be undertaken. Qualified counsellors should assist in the communication process. The following are suggested guidelines:

- develop the message so that it is delivered sensitively;
- two people should attend when delivering bad news;
- deliver the message as quickly and concisely as possible;

- if possible do not allow the receiver of bad news to go to the scene of the incident;
- arrange as soon as possible, monetary, welfare and counselling assistance; and
- stay in contact with victims after the incident.

# POST-TRAUMATIC STRESS

While there is no clear evidence that debriefing trauma victims is totally effective in reducing long-term problems, it has certainly been of great assistance in the short-term. Group debriefing has been seen as a one-off solution, but people directly affected in a tragedy may need a range of treatment, for example individual counselling. Post-traumatic stress disorder is characterised by frequent recollections of a traumatic event, emotional numbing and irritability, and can be associated with depression and, in some cases, substance abuse.

Disaster affects all those concerned, whether directly or indirectly. It is important to know about possible reactions to such unusual events, how to look after yourself, and how to help others. A crisis or disaster is usually unexpected and involves threat to life and welfare. Under these circumstances, it is normal to have an intense reaction, even from those only indirectly involved.

Reactions will include:

- shock—disbelief, numbness, difficulty in comprehension;
- body reactions—tension, trembling, sick stomach, weakness, loss of appetite, sweating and tiredness;
- thoughts—confusion, inability to concentrate, lack of clarity of thought;
- images—flashbacks, mistake familiar things for aspects of the disaster;
- emotions—fear, horror, sadness, irritability, anger, looking for someone to blame, apathy, loss of energy, helplessness, rapid changes of emotion, no longer feel safe anywhere;
- behaviour—highly aroused, inability to settle down, disturbed sleep, dreams and nightmares about the event, higher alcohol, cigarette and food intake;
- attitudes—bitterness, pessimism, feel somehow to blame, guilt at surviving or not being there, or not having done something, questioning of the meaning of life; and
- social—avoidance of people, irritable and intolerant, feel no-one understands, cannot let go of those who were involved.

These are all normal, common reactions of people in any kind of crisis or disaster, and are an attempt to adjust to what has happened. To a greater or lesser extent, these reactions may also be observed amongst members of the crisis management team. Sometimes these reactions do not happen until some time after the event. For this reason, counselling should be insisted upon, even when people consider they are 'okay'. Some form of professional counselling help is advisable to help those affected take charge of their own recovery.

## CONTROL POINTS

☐ Employees and victims' families must be told about crisis first and fast.

☐ Employees are an organisation's best allies if they are informed.

☐ Current systems are needed to contact employees after hours.

☐ Contractors must be linked to employee communication information networks.

☐ Counselling services should be available around the clock.

☐ If employees in other states or countries are affected by crisis, systems need to be in place to reach their family.

☐ Facilities need to be in place at every office, plant and site to deal with family inquiries.

☐ Welfare and support programs must be in place and monitored.

☐ Interpreters should be available if needed.

# 5

# EXTERNAL AUDIENCES

Almost immediately every telephone rang. 'What's wrong with your product?' And it was not just the consumer and the media. It was the government, the bureaucrats, consumer groups, academics, the trade and the industry. They all wanted facts. They all had comments. Hundreds of calls stressed the system in the first few hours. And the misperceptions kept coming. What was a simple product recall had become a massive case of misleading accusations. This famous family food product was being called a 'poisonous disaster'. There was an almost sustained program of false accusations and innuendo. It became a case of correcting and controlling the rumours and a need for source credibility to change the attitude of a wide group of audiences.

---

You have to get the message out. It is not just a case of sitting on your hands waiting for it all to go away. When a crisis hits, it is not time to walk, it is time to talk. A well-executed communication program to external audiences will play an important strategic role. Yet crisis communication is often mistakenly seen as no more than media releases. There are many vested interests which have to be carefully managed in order to retain strong confidence and support throughout the duration of a crisis. The management of the release of information and its continuity to audiences is the secret to controlling the response and preventing long-term damage to reputation and brand.

The TWA aircraft crash on 17 July 1996 that killed 230 passengers, captured the attention of millions of people and involved countless different groups of people. TWA badly fumbled the crisis response and the CEO ultimately lost his job. They just could not cope at TWA— they could not deal with the huge rate of inquiries from government, customers and distraught families. They could not cope with the intense media scrutiny and they could not handle the investigation.

This is the toughest kind of crisis. A large number of deaths, no warning and no clear reason. But there is an opportunity here to show how an organisation is prepared to talk, to get the message out quickly. One clear message to all stakeholders that the organisation does have a plan and is moving towards a resolution.

By contrast, in 1996 ValuJet, one of America's younger travel specialists, lost an aircraft in the Florida Everglades in the alligator-infested waters. One hundred and ten people died. ValuJet's Chairman, Lewis Jordan, led a massive communications approach of care and concern. They made every effort to keep their stakeholders informed from government at every level to customers affected, to families, to the community where the incident occurred. A policy of openness and a plan for managing a crisis was in place. ValuJet steadily recovered and maintenance staff were charged in 1999.

Who are your audiences in a crisis? It is essential to analyse and refine external crisis audiences well-ahead of a critical situation. Not just the people you expect to deal with, but the people you least expect to deal with. This could be a first time communication with special consumer groups, government investigation bodies, police tactical response groups, academic experts or representatives of community organisations. They all make up the essential crisis audience and they all require planned strategic response.

Some of these audiences can be dealt with by a trained telephone communicator with a planned message. Others will require a one-to-one pragmatic conversation. Keeping a tight hold and focus on your external audiences and pre-planning to reach those audiences with maximum impact will put you a long way ahead. Lack of planning and direction with external audiences may well result in the release of inaccurate information which can send your waiting audiences into an aggressive state of mind which, in turn, gives rise to a feeding frenzy from the media.

The terrorist attack on the World Trade Centre in New York created a whole new ball game of communication in the United States. This was urban terrorism head on for the full spectrum of emergency services. The whole purpose of terrorism, of course, is to disrupt systems and to create chaos—this is their victory. The more problems that are created with the more audiences, the more successful the act of terrorism.

There was a huge audience of people who needed to know—families, employees, neighbours—all of them waited for the flow of information and needed to know what really had happened. The Port Authority Executive Director, Stanley Brezenoff, became a spokesperson the minute he got out of the building. They planned to talk to everyone and they did it as fast as they could.

It was a time, too, for credible spokespeople from law enforcement agencies and rescue organisations. No-one really wants to hear from corporate spin doctors when they can get objective information from the FBI top dogs.

In 1998 the crew of the Australian navy ship, HMAS *Westralia*, had to take control. They had to respond immediately in managing a crisis at sea which tragically took four lives. What started off as an emergency incident with a fire breaking out, finished as a maritime crisis after a fireball tore through the ship's engine room.

The major issue was the Captain's decision to seal and flood the engine room with carbon dioxide. A quick assessment with a rapid response to control the situation. A clear statement of managing the problem based on training and field experience. Certainly head office or, in this case, naval headquarters, played a role in dealing with a wide range of crisis issues arising from the event.

But this naval crisis shows how much management systems can be put under stress. It shows how an emergency escalates to crisis. It also shows how exercises and rehearsals for emergencies and crises have to be part of a well-integrated plan.

It was not just a fire at sea that the navy had to face—it was the fallout of wider issues related to the tragic fatalities, safety issues and the decision-making process.

In any critical incident, the focus has to be on fast, efficient emergency response—fight the fire, save the lives. Equally there has to be focus on dealing with the wider crisis issues—the future of the operation, the effect on the community, handling employees, next of kin, and the management capacity to recover the business.

Immediately the navy had to deal with a whole set of urgent stakeholders—families, government at many and various levels, additional outside emergency services, other naval staff on board the HMAS *Westralia* as well as sailors, staff and officers on every Australian naval ship. There were academics making comments about decisions and fire retardants. There were ship designers and engineers. There were members of the government and bureaucrats. And of course there was the media—not just the day-to-day media but the front-page editorial media, the tough and determined investigative media—the talkback programs. All these audiences became involved as the emergency escalated to crisis.

Mercury power company in New Zealand seemed to have neither emergency nor crisis planning in place. Auckland's business district was plunged into darkness when the last of four major power cables supplying New Zealand's biggest city failed in February 1998.

As reported in *The Australian* newspaper, the day began with enormous confusion. While police and the fire service warned people to stay away from the city centre, mixed messages from employers and the determination of some retailers to stay open meant thousands turned up for work as usual. People gathered on the streets unsure of whether they would be working. Some businesses opened with loud-hailers and candles, while others remained closed.

Businesses affected by the crisis were demanding compensation from Mercury. The New Zealand government moved for a full inquiry. The crisis cost the economy tens of millions of dollars.

While it was all happening, when people wanted to know why the power was off, a Mercury spokesperson said there would be time to talk once power was restored. So Auckland waited to get the facts. This had all the characteristics of the worst kind of crisis management. Lack of comment and lack of response to consumer questions.

David Elias reported in the Melbourne *Age* 'Mercury Energy, the disaster-stricken electricity supplier at the centre of Auckland's power crisis, is facing a growing clamour for compensation and internal reform'.

The Mercury power company did not accept an invitation to address the businesses affected at the Auckland City Council. Eventually, while not openly admitting any liability, Mercury created a compensation fund to help businesses. But everybody waited too long to get the facts.

Did Mercury have a crisis plan linked to an emergency plan in case of total loss of power? It seems they did not.

## STAKEHOLDER EXTERNAL AUDIENCE GROUPS

In a control room at the time of a major disaster, there is a concentration on immediately contacting key audiences before they have to contact the organisation.

This proactivity is about getting ahead of your key audience agendas. It does not take long to call and tell a politician, a police officer, a media person, a regulator, a stockbroker, a banker or a counsellor about your emerging problem and how you are dealing with it. They become a credible source in spreading the word. It's not a time to bury your head in the sand and say nothing. The bunker mentality may feel good for a few hours but it is the fastest way to encourage the rumour mill.

The court of public opinion wants to know what happened. Very quickly they will make a decision as to whether you are guilty or not guilty. If they can see that you are dealing with the situation and making every effort to fix it, they will come on side.

Commercial Union, one of Britain's largest insurance companies, had their offices in London blown apart as a result of a terrorist bombing in 1992. Much of the crisis control was handled by the City of London Police in a very efficient manner, however the company played their part in dealing with a large group of audiences. The CEO and crisis team leader split the business management team into two, one to deal with the day-to-day running of the business and the other to deal with the crisis.

This explosion killed 3 people and injured 30. Four hundred tons of glass and debris were spread across the street and the City of London was brought to a virtual standstill. The Commercial Union premises were totally inoperable. The management team went straight to their crisis plan which outlined crisis management teams and established priorities.

As part of their damage limitation, assessment and action planning, they were quickly able to audit their employees to identify injured people and make contact with families. They had procedures for effective liaison with emergency services. Plans were in place for the safety of their building and security of their company's information and equipment. They also had an inventory and control for removal of equipment and information.

All meetings and discussions were documented. They moved straight into recovery mode to restore communication links and it was not long before they had established alternative premises and replacement of their main switchboard and computer information facilities. They established a temporary communications centre, while they were moving into their new building, and they were able to follow a plan of where to go, what to do and who does what.

They made themselves available and distributed information to their staff, the public, media, customers, shareholders, brokers and the insurance industry. Commercial Union particularly honed in on immediate and longer-term plans for staff to encourage morale, goodwill and enthusiasm.

Admittedly, Commercial Union were the victims of a terrorist bomb that blew up outside their 23-storey building. They certainly had the support and understanding of the British population behind them. However, regardless of this support, they had to ensure company and corporate survival at the same time as showing that they were able to manage the situation. They were able to ensure continuity of operations and control of the situation.

The sheer volume of calls in a crisis situation requires systems to be set up that clearly demonstrate the company is ready to answer inquiries and to deal with the important calls (see Figure 5.1). The basic principle applied must be to identify the operational from the non-operational inquiries.

Calls from police, rescue services or emergency response should be directed to the designated co-ordinator in the crisis management team. Non-operational inquiries should be passed on to the public affairs co-ordinator of the crisis management team, who can decide rapidly on the relevance of the inquiry and who should deal with it. These calls may well end up with the crisis team leader or the CEO.

*Figure 5.1* Crisis stakeholders

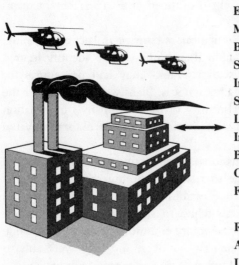

Employees
Employee families
Media
Board of Directors
Shareholders
Investment community
Special interest groups
Local communities
International community
Banks, insurers
Customers
Federal, State and Local
    government
Regulatory authorities
Academics
Unions

**Table 5.1** *The field of crisis audiences*

| | | |
|---|---|---|
| **Government** | Bankers | Environmental groups |
| Politicians | Analysts | Religious groups |
| Bureaucrats | Institutions | Community groups |
| Regulators | **Insurers** | Academic and |
| Investigators | Property | education groups |
| **Media** | Workers' compensation | **Customers and Suppliers** |
| National | Risk | Customers directly |
| Financial | **International** | affected |
| Regional | Joint venturers | Potential customers |
| Local | Governments | **Emergency Services** |
| Print | Communities | Local and Federal |
| Television – general | **Industry** | police organisations |
| and investigative | Organisations | Fire and rescue services |
| Radio | Unions | Medical and ambulance |
| Publications | Professional and trade | Security support groups |
| Internet | associations | Forensic and |
| **Financial Community** | **Special Interest Groups** | psychology services |
| Stock Exchange | Neighbours | |
| Shareholders/investors | Consumer groups | |

## MANAGING THE MEDIA

Bad news makes headlines. And no matter where you are today, the media is never very far away. It takes only moments to beam the news into our homes from isolated locations.

And crises have become spectator sports. We are a world of watchers. After all, millions of viewers watched the world-shattering royal crisis in Paris when Diana, Princess of Wales and Dodi Al-Fayed were killed in a horrific car crash. We watched Stuart Diver, the lone survivor, being gently cradled to safety at Thredbo after a mountainside collapsed in an Australian ski resort killing 19 people. And we watched O. J. Simpson drive recklessly down the LA Freeway for 3 hours following the much publicised death of his ex-wife and her friend. Ted Turner's CNN has made crisis essential viewing since the Gulf War.

In a mining crisis recently, men trapped deep underground were speaking on talkback radio live to their wives about their impending rescue. The company involved had to deal with the speed and safety of the rescue as well as the speed of the message coming from under-ground. Technology has compressed time. Opinions are formed in minutes.

And rumour will run the agenda unless there is a plan. It was rumour that ran the agenda in the early stages of the Oklahoma bomb blast. First images and first blame was laid at the feet of terrorists from the Middle East. Rumour has it that a Middle Eastern 'type' ran from the building shortly before the blast. Later the FBI charged a local group.

In the early hours of the disastrous Mercedes crash in the Paris tunnel, some television reports indicated that the Princess of Wales only had a few scratches and mild concussion. The media had problems of reporting a disaster that was sealed off in a tunnel with few witnesses. Rumour ran riot with a battle of agendas being waged by a number of stakeholders including the French authorities, the British government and the spin doctors of the Al-Fayed business interests.

It is the 'speed of events' that organisations involved in a serious situation have to face. In crisis, it is the tyranny of time controlled by the media. We will call it 'instant agenda' control.

Some people say this instant agenda control was started by the television news media in Vietnam as they followed the actions of war. But film footage had to be shipped to Hong Kong from Saigon. The BBC presented the news of the 1982 Falklands war to the rest of the world by using file footage over and over again. The first real live television war was the Persian Gulf War of 1991. Live television on CNN came from behind the lines via satellite straight into a huge worldwide audience at home.

More often than not, in a crisis situation, an organisation needs the media as much as the media needs it. While there may be fears of your spokesperson cornered outside your building with a barrage of microphones and cameras and loads of unanswerable questions, and thoughts of replayed news clips and sound bites, it does not have to be this way. With the right planning, bad news can be turned to your advantage.

Controlling the media is about controlling the message. If you are proactive and positive, then your good news will be given just as much time as your bad news.

In the midst of the worst possible accident, explosion, crash, spill or product recall, there is much to be said about positive things that are being done to improve the situation. The sooner these things are said and done, the faster the perception becomes a reality.

In 1980, Procter & Gamble worked with the media when its 'Rely' tampons were related to toxic shock. The product was recalled rapidly and information was passed to the consumer through press, radio and television. Procter & Gamble did all it could to make this issue news and show that it was concerned about public health. This communication strategy related to its product recall protected both the brand reputation and saved the company from what may have been huge liability suits.

Media management is a skilled task, requiring knowledge, experience and sensitivity. There should be only one point of contact for the media within the company during a crisis, and that should be the nominated spokesperson. So, while individual locations may need to prepare and present holding statements, it should be the responsibility of head office to provide official statements at the time of any crisis and this should be delivered by the CEO. Setting up a plan for managing the media during a crisis involves developing a set of guidelines for the media spokesperson and co-ordinator, in liaison with the company's corporate affairs department or its equivalent. Such guidelines and procedures for responding to the news media must be established and clearly understood throughout the organisation, so there can be no deviation when the media onslaught begins.

Each crisis must be handled as the response dictates. While a range of contingency statements will be prepared for media and employees, the objective remains the same—to ensure the communication of timely, accurate and consistent information.

With all the confusion surrounding a crisis, crisis management teams may be tempted to push media communications aside until all the facts are known. However, news of a crisis can be received from any number of channels, and delay can be costly in terms of controlling the message.

Pre-crisis procedures should include:

- identifying the media and drawing up key lists of radio, television and press outlets that are likely to cover the crisis both initially and in the longer-term;

- preparation of background information—seize the initiative by keeping updated background information packs about various sites with diagrams and any positive material which can help the reporter understand your operations;

- conducting operational and plant tours and occasional briefings with specialist journalists;

- training key spokespersons in the handling of media interviews under crisis conditions;

- setting up a briefing/training program for receptionists and telephonists, so as to maintain effective control of all incoming and outgoing calls and media enquiries during a crisis; and

- instigating a media call register.

Crisis communication should include:

- Assembling necessary information. This should cover: the effect of the event on employees, the cause of the event, background information as to the cause, event location at the site, strategy being employed to control the crisis.
- Preparation of a media standby or holding statement. This should be done immediately and then regularly updated as facts become available.
- Preparation should be made for the media visiting the location of the incident and the various offices of the organisation. Personnel should be briefed to escort the media to a suitable location. If a press conference is required, rooms should be prepared with suitable lecterns, seating, power and interview space.
- The company's media spokesperson needs to be briefed on the current situation and the main points that need to be made about the situation. The information that most reporters will want to find out in a crisis situation is:
  What's happening now?
  How will it affect the people involved?
  What is the scale and the cost of it?
  What are the problems related to the recovery?
  Who is in controlling the situation?
  Why did it happen?
  What are you doing about it?

Post-crisis procedures should include:

- continuing to update media on all aspects of the recovery; and
- reviewing media exposure and dealing with a broad range of 'people' issues arising out of the event.

## GOVERNMENTS AND BUREAUCRATS

Nobody can afford to ignore government during a crisis or hope that they will not get involved, because they will. A major challenge for every organisation in a crisis is fast access to government at all levels.

In one of the world's worst environmental crises, where the *Exxon Valdez* tanker spewed millions of gallons of oil into Prince William Sound in Alaska, the President of the United States ordered the coastguard in to manage the clean up. This unprecedented government intervention came after a series of offers of government assistance was refused by Exxon management. And these government offers of assistance were not just from departments of the US government, they also came from the Netherlands, Norway and the former Soviet Union. The US Oil Pollution Act now clearly states that government will play a major part in managing all future disasters of this nature.

The growth of environmental protection, consumerism, product safety management, higher standards of occupational health and safety, responsibilities and accountabilities in the boardroom, and community standards all involve government legislation. Increasing consumer awareness and tougher legislation means the government needs to know immediately there is a problem so they can, in many cases, work with the organisation to help shape an effective response. The government can be a vital ally and back-up, a source of information, support and advice.

Critical to the management of a crisis is a comprehensive and well-executed communication program with government at all levels. In most cases, this government contact will be made by the existing government liaison channels.

It is important to consider, however, that many areas and levels of government have statutory compliance, regulatory or investigative issues uppermost in their agendas, and will require specific processes, powers and responsibilities to be enacted.

For example, natural disasters and terrorist acts automatically become the crisis management responsibility of government under the laws of most countries. Producers of hazardous materials or toxic by-products must submit to strict containment and emergency standards and generally their disaster plans are mandated.

The Emergency Planning and Right to Know Act in US law outlines the process for emergency plans under the following components:

- identification of facilities and transportation routes that contain hazardous substances;
- emergency response procedures to be used on the site and surrounding areas;
- identification of personnel designated as the community and facility co-ordinators responsible for implementing the plan;
- procedures for notifying authorities and potentially affected parties;
- methods for determining when a release has occurred and the probable area (and population) that could be at risk;

- descriptions of the emergency equipment and facilities available in the community; and

- plans for evacuating facilities and potentially affected areas.

In the case of a serious product recall related to a design defect or criminal contamination, legislation varies from country to country but firm laws related to electrical appliances, motor vehicles, food and pharmaceuticals, are being applied to prevent dangerous products being further produced or distributed.

In the United States, the Consumer Product Safety Commission and the Food and Drug Administration are amongst the major government bodies that have to be notified immediately once the risk of injury or the severity of possible injury or both is suspected to be substantial, or if applicable mandatory standards or regulations are violated. The Food and Drug Administration, in particular, is in the position to force a product recall depending on the severity of the circumstances.

In Australia, the Trade Practices Act gives the relevant government minister the power to ban the supply of unsafe goods and order suppliers to recall consumer goods with safety related defects and issue public warning notices.

The United Nations General Assembly has published standards on consumer protection, encouraging governments to adopt appropriate measures including legal systems and safety regulations, national or international standards and voluntary standards to ensure that products are safe for intended or normally foreseeable use.

In the case of criminal contamination, extortion, hostage, kidnapping or acts of terrorism, most countries have strict laws related to the involvement of the country's law enforcement agencies. Working with government to prepare contingency plans for dealing with such situations is an essential part of crisis planning. Knowing where to get help, which department to go to and which people to talk to needs to be firmly established. Procedures need to be identified and key players who have the authority to act confirmed.

The company Geothermal, part of Union Oil, US, in the Philippines, had no crisis plan for kidnap or ransom. Their CEO, Michael Barnes, was kidnapped by the Red Scorpion crime group in January 1992. The group demanded US$25 million. Barnes was held for 60 gruelling, horrific days. He was rescued when police stormed the kidnappers' hideout—there was a shoot-out that killed 14 people. The trauma from that incident caused major disruption to that business. Interaction with Government was vital.

## THE GOVERNMENT GAME PLAN

Managing government relations in a crisis requires a contingency plan to assure effective communication:

* anticipate the government departments that will be involved in any crisis threat;
* provide contact with the leaders of those government departments;
* communicate crisis management strategy and methodology;
* identify processes, powers and responsibilities of each person and department;
* develop government assistance guidelines in line with government policy; and
* involve and rehearse government liaison in crisis exercises.

This government game plan needs to be a dedicated process and not tacked on to other public policy projects. It should encourage positive thinking and focus on effective recovery and business continuity. It is important to include a conflict resolution factor in the process in order to eliminate difficult issues well-ahead of a crisis event.

## KEEPING WATCH— ENVIRONMENTALISTS AND SPECIAL INTEREST GROUPS

If environmentalists existed in the old days of London pea souper fogs, then inner city life may have changed a lot earlier. The most devastating of the fogs took place in 1952. It took the death of 4000 people in the worst fog and pollution disaster the world has ever witnessed to introduce London's strict environmental regulations. Parliament immediately voted to set up an Emergency Atmospheric Pollution Committee to investigate the problems of air pollution. It was given power to examine the almost non-existent, anti-pollution control and ensure that a disaster on such a scale would never happen again.

The environmental organisation, Greenpeace, was conceived in 1971, when members of the 'Don't Make a Wave Committee' in Vancouver, Canada, renamed their organisation. Greenpeace embraces environmental protection and highlights illegal trade in toxic waste and abuse of the environment.

Greenpeace, and many other environmental protection organisations that have followed their style, have a fast communication network to the world's media, politicians and other similar groups.

They were one of the first special interest groups to take advantage of the Internet and today provide a wide range of information on environmental issues and environmental protection initiatives.

In the 1970s and 1980s, a number of disastrous environmental crises forever changed the way governments and business viewed environmental performance. Specialists in green standards hung out their signs in almost every country in the world and society began to understand that environmental protection was part of everyday life.

A decade before the devastating Union Carbide plant explosion at Bhopal in India, there was a shocking disaster midway between Milan and Lake Como in Italy. In a little town called Sevesco, an explosion occurred at the Icmesa chemical plant that created a huge dust cloud above the village. The next day, trees and plants began to die, small animals collapsed and died and the children of the town developed horrific sores on their arms and legs. It was some days later that the management of Icmesa, owned by a huge Swiss drug company, agreed that the cloud was caused by a freak chemical cocktail tetrachlorodibenzodioxin, or the defoliant ingredient used by the United States in Vietnam. Hundreds of people were affected and today, the area is a contaminated ghost town of desolation.

While organisations worldwide build new and responsible environmental strategies, the crisis management of environmental incidents and disasters requires a firm foundation. Senior management needs to work closer with environmental specialists to identify environmental threats and confirm their capability of responding effectively in terms of both human and technical resources.

There has to be a clear set of guidelines as a point of reference and the methodology to be used, both in the response and the investigation, has to be mutually in accord with regulations and specialists. And the organisation's performance in response has to be clear, precise and believable.

The key to good environmental crisis management is that perception often has very little to do with reality. You can have the best environmental policy and clean-up team in the world, but if you are not perceived to be on top of the response, then you will lose the match and suffer the reputational consequences.

## THE FINANCIAL GURUS

A major difficulty encountered during a crisis is the continual build up of concern by an organisation's financial audiences. It is essential to get on top of your financial audience before they are led by business analysts, academics and financial journalists.

Even the famous Nintendo video game can be affected by crisis. Six hundred children were reported to have suffered vomiting, convulsions and other symptoms when the video game *Pocket Monsters* created a 'bright red explosion on screens'. Nintendo shares dipped noticeably following the Nintendo organisation's statement that it did not expect the incident to have any impact on its business.

The Australian company, Pacific Dunlop, who market a wide range of products, diversified into Telectronics pacemakers. In 1996, the pacemakers were recalled following the discovery of a faulty lead wire after the death of two patients. The class action that followed would potentially cover some 9000 patients. PacDun sold Telectronics as the threat of multi-million dollar lawsuits remained. At the same time, they sold their A$1.1 billion food operations to focus on their core business.

While they continually briefed analysts and fund managers during these events, the financial markets and business journalists continued to cast doubts on the company's performance and the share price fell dramatically. The pacemaker problem became a thorn in the side of the company alongside its departure from the food industry and as the share price continued to plummet, the CEO departed.

Even if not directly concerning finance, a major product recall can lead to crisis where negative reports by financial analysts and stockbrokers can lead to unwanted coverage in the financial media. From there it is only a short step to the general news pages of a newspaper. And a run on your share price has begun before you are ready for it.

Sophisticated audiences in the world of finance will need sophisticated responses that explain without evasion and clarify without confusion. The corporate watchdogs spread across innumerable government agencies will also need credible, convincing and transparent answers.

## NEW TECHNOLOGY

Getting ahead of the technology race should be high on the agenda of a crisis manager. There are many excellent opportunities now to improve communications capability with new state-of-the-art communication tools.

Portability will be the key. Powerful personal organisers that link into a total network through a modem are an enormous asset to a crisis team that has to work in a distant location. It won't be long before these organisers can integrate faxes, Internet capability and even live video conferencing into the system. It means that crisis teams will be able to take miniature cameras right into the crisis scene and send live pictures back to head office. In turn, head office crisis management teams will be able to send urgent information on employees and customers straight down the line as audit trail checklists for the crisis management team on the spot of a crisis to use.

The Internet will come into its own as the public uses the Net to gain information about issues that concern them. Commerce will in turn look at the worldwide web as a way to reach its audiences rapidly in times of difficulty.

In a recent survey of journalists in the USA, they were asked what they would do in the case of a major crisis or disaster—where would they go for urgent background information details. A very large proportion of the journalists questioned suggested they would look for a web site for the company or organisation affected.

In 1996, a tragedy occurred on a routine ascent at the mighty Mt Everest. While more than 30 climbers were descending, eight died and three were seriously affected by frostbite. This famous mountain, with its history of extraordinary feats and achievements, once again became an item of world news. But this time, the Internet played a part in both confirming information and as a medium for which the families of victims could turn to for mutual grieving.

*Time* magazine covered the story in an article called 'Death Breaks Live on the Web' by Julie K.L. Darn, reported by Jenifer Mattos, New York (1996):

"By midday Saturday, the Internet was buzzing over the real-time updates that trickled in from the climbers and rescuers via satellite phone and fax. Outside On Line saw its traffic quadruple a day after the blizzard. NBC's site had more than 1 000 000 visits on Monday alone. Full coverage of the mishap did not appear in *The New York Times* until Tuesday. 'This is the first major international news story that broke live on the Web', says Marty Yudkovitz, President of NBC Interactive Media. 'It tells of the added dimensions the Internet can bring to journalism.

"The web sites also proved invaluable to relatives and friends. Outside On Line established a chat area—editors called it the grieving room, where people could share information."

While crisis discussions in cyberspace could face problems because of the very public nature of the medium and, as *Time* suggested, news flashing over the Internet that is both unfiltered and unconfirmed, could be wrong. But the facts of life are that the medium is certainly faster than the newspaper and because of its ability to be broadcast from the most extreme locations, it is faster than live television or radio.

If there is any doubt that the Internet is a major tool for mass communications then it was confirmed for all time in the frenzied blast of information about the President of the United States and his sex life that appeared on the Net.

First of all, the information about Bill Clinton's activities with Monica Lewinsky appeared in a gossip column called *The Drudge Report* which claims to have about 7 million hits a month and 100 000 e-mail subscribers including a large number of senior journalists and government officials.

It apparently used a tip leaked from *Newsweek* magazine's news room about the sexual encounters and possible tapes. Then it moved to every mainstream television, radio and newspaper around the world. All the detail followed of Ken Starr, the First Lady, the Grand Jury, other members of government and Congress. The Internet pushed the news out, taking every possible angle. The world was double-clicking for more of the main menu. Some major web sites included video clips of the now famous Clinton hug at a re-election rally and also portions of Linda Tripp's notes. There were even Monica Lewinsky fan pages on the web and a web page supposedly run by Lewinsky herself. It was called *Monica's Place*, featuring the Shakespeare quotation: "Oh what a tangled web we weave".

While the web has played a major part in the speed of the story, it is fair to say that it is the major newspapers that have become the authority behind the story. *Newsweek, The Washington Post, The Los Angeles Times* and *The New York Times* have given extensive and careful background of the story. It is this depth of background by the newspapers and, in most cases, the television stations, that the public has turned to for a better understanding of this late twentieth century Presidential crisis.

It needs to be reiterated that while the web has been responsible for bringing the story to light, it has been the mainstream quality press that has perhaps assisted in leading the majority of the US public to the view that the President should survive.

In the last few years mobile phones have been a major breakthrough in providing rapid assistance and information during a crisis, but of course mobile phones have to be within reach of a network.

The new iridium satellite telephone will provide instant communication from anywhere in the world and will become a must for any crisis management team on the move. It operates without telephone lines or network cellular systems. It relies on 66 low orbit satellites that are in constant earth orbit.

Calls will cost several dollars a minute but this remarkable telephone, that is not much bigger than a normal mobile phone, with a slightly more expanded aerial, is around $5000.

The other useful device for crisis teams operating away from base will be a series of software programs that will provide immediate support checklists for crisis situations. The software will offer preprepared media releases, audit trailed response checklists for each team member and essential contact numbers and support advice. There is also software that provides comprehensive business impact analysis for recovery, including complete crisis recovery plans and automated PC-based recovery.

The Gulf War introduced a number of new devices that have been taken on by crisis and disaster teams. One is called a Global Positioning Satellite portable, which teams can carry with them to any kind of location. It is now being seriously considered as a major asset for aircraft, yachts and explorers. This mobile Global Positioning Satellite Receiver is priced between $100 and $1500.

## CONTROL POINTS

☐ Analysing and refining crisis audiences needs to be done ahead of a critical situation.

☐ What is said can be strategically planned ahead.

☐ Controlling the high ground is about delivering key messages fast.

☐ Technology has compressed time. Opinions are formed in minutes.

☐ Rumour will run the agenda unless there is a plan.

☐ Being proactive and positive will be good news in the face of bad news.

☐ Media management is a skilled task requiring experience and sensitivity.

☐ Organisations need to plan their government response ahead of a crisis identifying processes, powers and responsibilities.

☐ Involve and rehearse government liaison in crisis exercises.

☐ Environmentalists and special interest groups require priority consideration in crisis management planning.

☐ Financial academics and journalists are an essential audience in corporate crisis strategy.

☐ New portable technology will win the communication agenda—the Internet, iridium satellite phones, crisis software and Global Positioning Satellite receivers.

# 6

# COMMUNICATING ACTIONS

His long time friend, partner and director of the company had been arrested the night before. The charge was fraud and four other managers had gone down with him. The company was still solid and its products leading the field, in fact until now, everything was moving upwards. The defence of the corporation and everything this CEO believed in was a priority. Now more than ever, he needed his public relations people to help tell the real story. But the rumours had started. The queue of media was growing fast and they were not just the columnists but more the hard-headed investigative journalists who needed to dig deep. There could only be one star of this show and it had to be him. He had to give the performance of a lifetime.

In hippocratic medicine, crisis means the actual time when a disease reaches a final point. Most people know that if you can control a medical emergency effectively in the first few minutes or hours, then you can save a life. This is very much the same situation in the resolution of the early moments of a crisis. Gaining control of the media agenda prevents much of the fear and apprehension surrounding the situation. This takes charge of the message agenda and retains the initiative to lead the information flow.

Do not blame the media. Crises are news and there are hundreds of very professional journalists who must get the facts to satisfy their public. They are doing their job and, if you were not involved in the crisis, you would expect them to give you the news. All too often journalists are blamed for being too intrusive. But, if they do not give us the facts, we soon ask why.

Of course the media is interested and if they cannot get it immediately, they will go somewhere else. They must have a spokesperson to lead their story. The prospect of taking the media spotlight by doing an interview may strike terror into the heart of most corporate leaders, however, it must be one of their first priorities. There seems to be a mind-set in some management circles that by providing the media with facts early on, they are going to be accused of mayhem. It is just the opposite. Every fact that you provide in the early stages will release the pressure off both the spokesperson and the internal stakeholders.

In the case of one therapeutic products company during an escalating product recall, the leading network's 'warrior' interviewer demanded he spoke to the Chief Executive so he could get the news 'right from the horse's mouth'. He shouted down the telephone that there would be hell to pay if the company did not come good and give the network the story. 'I will stand outside your plant with the company name in the background,' he shouted, 'and tell the story as I see it until you submit.'

The CEO was experienced in media interviews and took on the task of meeting the 'warrior'. His organisation's image and, to a degree, his reputation, was on the line. Certainly there was going to be some difficulty in getting the message across and there would be traps and perhaps his words would be twisted, but he had to tell the story.

Well, this CEO met the 'warrior' and turned the setback into a springboard. Questions were asked about the quality of the product and its future in the marketplace. The CEO positioned the product as essential and vital to saving lives and identified the problem in the product recall as being controllable and the company as being in control of that problem. He offered cool, clear and instant advice to the public about how to get information on the situation and by the end of the interview, he had total clarity on the company's confident approach to managing the situation. He retained the initiative throughout and was never outmanoeuvred. The sad end to this story of investigative dynamics was that the interview was never used. Was it too good to be true or too true to be good?

For the uninitiated, a period of media attack can be disastrous. A barrage of cameras, microphones and tape recorders coming at you from every angle. How do you avoid being ambushed by the early questions and how do you contain the situation without looking like you are on the defensive? You understand what the media will want well before an incident occurs. You plan, prepare and practise.

The Radio and Television News Directors' Association in the United States was surveyed in 1996 on media expectations of an organisation during a crisis or disaster. They wanted to find out how television stations covered an incident. They also interviewed people from the public relations industry who had been involved in a crisis. The most important responses were to the question of 'when a crisis occurs, how often does your organisation want updated information?'. The most frequent answers were 'constantly', 'immediately' and 'as soon as possible'. Respondents to the research also wrote 'as soon as new developments warrant the public being informed'.

An interesting byline to this research was that 98 of 133 responding television stations did not have a plan to cover the event during the last organisational crisis or serious disaster that they covered. The only real plan they had was that the reporters got out there and got the story first and fast.

What does all this mean to most organisations? It simply says that you can win the war of words—that you do have the opportunity of being better prepared to deal with a crisis situation than other stakeholders. You can control the agenda.

It is true to say that a picture is worth a thousand words. They still say that the South Vietnamese general putting the gun to the head of a captured North Vietnamese soldier and summarily executing him in the street had such enormous impact on the world news that it was the trigger that ended the war in Vietnam.

In the case of the Shell UK Group, they were simply going to get rid of the Brent Spar oil rig in the North Sea in 1993. Everybody was seemingly happy. They had the approval of the British government and there had been continual discussion with environmentalists and the community. Then just when everything seemed to be in order, and the engineers were ready to remove the oil rig, Greenpeace protesters landed on the deck of the oil rig. Shell went into action and aimed their water cannons at the intruders.

What did the world see at Brent Spar when a helicopter piloted by a woman attempted to put Greenpeace protesters on the deck of the oil rig? Protesters defending their right on the deck of the Brent Spar under attack by high-powered water cannons of the massive multinational. The *Wall Street Journal* said: 'Shell had made a strategic error. In a world of sound bites ... one image was left with many viewers. A huge multinational oil company was mustering all its might to bully what was portrayed as a brave but determined band.'

# THE BEST APPROACH

There are many different approaches to media training and most of them concentrate on how to make the best out of any media appearance opportunity. In other words, you always accept, seldom decline and put your best foot forward. This is far from the case because there are times when you must decline an interview, regardless of all that has been said in previous chapters of being first and being fast. There are times when a spokesperson has to say no. There are also spokespeople who should never be spokespeople. Some people are not cut out to be on the receiving end of an interview.

Let us deal with these issues in order. First of all, look at this scenario. A room full of people asking for an interview at a time when you have to tell your story and you have been given sufficient information to deal with most of the key questions from the media. Then all of a sudden, the most obnoxious voice from the corner of the room asks you some unrelated and personal question: 'What will your family think of you now?' or 'How can you hold your head up in public after this?'. These sorts of questions should be dealt with swiftly with the answers, 'I won't answer that, it's not relevant' or 'Let's move on to a question related to the incident'.

This scenario can be applied to the interview request. It is likely that a spokesperson will be requested to do an interview with a journalist who only wants the dirt, who is known for strongarm tactics and can frankly do neither the spokesperson or the cause any good at all. It could be argued that this person represents the top rating program, but at a time of great pressure—when the company's reputation is on the line—you need to deal with an exchange of information not scuttlebutt. Sure, you need to expect your argument to be tested and at times to have a pretty serious cross-examination on the problem, but you do not need a manipulative rumour monger making things worse. Their view of the crisis is basically to find weaknesses in the leadership and pull down individuals. They are looking for someone to blame.

So, always be available in a crisis but never be pressurised into doing an interview with a journalist who is purely setting out to fill his or her ego agenda. This sort of journalist will already have a reputation for concentrating on the negative. So there will be an advance warning. At a time of crisis, whether the organisation is at fault or the threat is from outside, you will have the mass media waiting in the wings. You will be in demand. In most cases, you will also have the choice as to whom you wish to do interviews with and which questions you answer.

Do you or do you not avoid those high-rating current affairs programs that put your opponents or your victims into debate with you? Your defence will be tested and emotions will be running high. You certainly should not do this interview in the early stages of a crisis —you will not have time and you may not have the facts.

Concentrate on the main media of the day and continue to enunciate the key messages. As the crisis moves through the response phase, and you have begun to deal with recovery, then that is a good time to spend explaining what the company is doing to help people. This is also an opportunity for you to be very clear-sighted about your organisation's response related to the human issues.

Every CEO or senior manager is not necessarily a great spokesperson. Now most trainers will tell you that good salespeople are not born, they are made. Good spokespeople cannot be made if they do not have the right in-built communication skills in the first place. A spokesperson should not only be able to speak but they must be able to be understood by an audience. Being understood is as much about how something is said and how the person delivering the message is seen. So you can have the most intelligent person in the world in charge of some very important facts, but if they are stumbling, fumbling, jumpy, nervous and ill at ease, then the message is diminished.

Anger is seen as unprofessional, and people who lose their cool in a crisis give enormous comfort to the media who are looking for a weak spot. Such a person is easily lulled into a false sense of security, which weakens their response to criticism and then their prevarication gives a clear picture of bluff.

Back to the silent and unsure type. This uncomfortable spokesperson can be sent to the Royal Academy of Dramatic Art and given a serious course on dramatic rhythm and auditory composition, but while their oral interpretation may improve, the overall visual concept of their presentation remains a non-event. So with today's audiences demanding strong spokesperson communicators, who are able to leap tall crises at a single bound and communicate faster than a speeding cameraperson, what do you do in a crisis? Simple—you find a spokesperson at or near the top who can do the job well, very well.

And that spokesperson, with the greatest of respect to those wordsmiths and ex-news presenters-cum-public affairs officers, should not be a member of public affairs, public relations or internal media staff. Why? Most people know they wrote the script and are hired to 'spin' it right and therefore they are simply not believable. The public affairs professional is, without doubt, a valuable communication 'stage manager' in any crisis. He or she is a bridge builder who understands the needs of the audience and the requirements of the media.

Some organisations believe these people should be spokespeople and encourage it. But they understand little about public perception and the reality of the customer. Putting a public affairs person up as a spokesperson in a crisis situation or in any situation is no different to asking a politician whether his or her party is the best.

The right spokesperson needs to be comfortable and in control. Most of all, they have to be confident about delivering positive messages in the face of a crisis. Most news people want the facts and, frankly, this is what a good spokesperson has to be able to give in simple language. But they not only have to sound cool, calm and confident, they have to look it.

They also have to be prepared to dominate in the delivery of the agenda over that of the reporter. They have to talk the language of action and describe what the organisation is doing for people, because while most spokespeople may have in their mind the protection of their share price and the company's future, the general public watching the 6.00 p.m. news is interested in the human issues.

Generally speaking, all crisis spokespeople have to deal with the impact the incident has created. The interview has to be relevant and deal with the issues. If the answers play down the real situation, the organisation and the spokesperson is making it hard on themselves. What are the five key issues that have to be dealt with in every crisis statement and interview?

1. Human life and concern
   Reassure the media that all lives are safe and there is no threat to the environment or that you are doing everything possible to save both.
2. The current situation
   Bring the media up-to-date with the current situation. Answer all their questions so they go away content and not likely to fossick for further information.
3. Credibility through concern
   Restore and/or maintain credibility by expressing concern for what has happened.

4.  Accurate facts and figures
    Provide accurate facts and figures. If you are not sure, say so and say you will provide them with the correct information as soon as possible.
5.  What are you doing about the problem?
    Confirm your response actions.

## SERIOUS MEDIA TRAINING

What is the best kind of media training for a crisis? If ever a serious communication course was needed, then this is it. Strategies for effectively managing interviews and conferences in the wake of an emergency or a crisis is something that is seldom taught. Most media training programs touch on the bright lights, dressing for the part and knowing the answers to the questions. There are dozens of ex-journalists and interviewers who run training sessions for CEOs and senior managers on improving confidence and lifting interview technique.

Nothing wrong with this sort of training providing all those executives are doing chat shows—talking about their services and their products and generally 'chewing the fat'. But a serious crisis media training program must address agenda control and the delivery of central messages.

The setting for any crisis is chaotic. The spokesperson does not have time for a training session. There is no time for setting the location up or rehearsing dozens of likely questions and answers. All the spokesperson can do in a crisis is get the main points over at the same time as giving the most persuasive performance.

How do you train for delivering a message in the chaos of a crisis? You not only analyse your vulnerabilities and determine the effects of your business, but you look at what you will say and how you will say it when and if a crisis happens. The specialised training for crisis is not about answering questions, it is about running agendas. The training should concentrate on delivering messages in short and simple points to a strict agenda.

The spokesperson should understand about delivering messages of confidence and sympathy. They should learn about delivering messages quickly and efficiently. It is more about the process of communication that becomes the training ground than the actual delivery. It is also about preparing concise answers. In these days of the instant news grab, longwinded statements are useless.

# HIT LIST FOR HANDLING
# CRISIS INTERVIEWS

There is no point in presenting detailed executive guidelines to handling the media in this publication, however there seems to be some value in reviewing the key issues related to taking control and turning the interview towards your agenda.

- Do the interview sooner rather than later.
- Avoid sit-down interviews. Stand up and deliver.
- Be proactive—give the right facts before they suggest the wrong ones.
- Start with a statement of sympathy.
- Link your actions with those of the authorities.
- Don't tell lies.
- Stay calm and positive and show you are in total control of both the situation and the interview.
- Get your main points across at the start—live interviews are fast.
- Be brief in all your answers.
- Correct any misinformation or negative statements in the introduction or close.
- Do not respond to rumour, innuendo or information you are not aware of.
- Finish the interview before it finishes you.

So when faced by an angry or urgent media, stand your ground. Maybe they are coming at you like a pack of wolves or waiting for the grab on the steps of your lobby. Here is what you do:

- Make short, concise statements to one person in the group.
- Answer all questions with one or two prepared statements.
- Do not use jargon and do not apportion the blame.
- Tell them you will get back to them as soon as further information has been gathered.
- Finish, then leave the journalists with the clear impression that you are the only spokesperson.

Importantly, in a crisis, people are looking for positive leadership, therefore the statement must be said in a positive way without sounding vague or unsure. It is important not to be forced into making statements when you are not ready. You can certainly seek out the media's assistance in your task to resolve the current problem.

Statements such as 'we appreciate your support and hope that this message is getting through to the people who are affected' or 'with your help I would like to give a special emergency number of 00-44-44. People can call this for assistance'.

No spokesperson, if they are doing their job well, gives long interviews. They should be short, precise and limited to the key information. The best excuse you will ever have for finishing an interview is the fact that you have to get back to the crisis situation. 'You must excuse me now ... there is much to be done but I will return to give you an update in 45 minutes.'

## PRESS CONFERENCES

The other essential element in media training is the press conference. In the most serious emergencies and disasters, the press conference becomes an essential part of message delivery. It is an opportunity to deliver one message to a large number of media people in one hit. A press conference requires a special room and a specific set-up to accommodate camera crews, broadcast journalists and press.

It does take a lot of room for additional support media to write and transmit their copy, to talk to their news room, to deal with editing and to do live updates by mobile telephone. And if the incident is prolonged they will be eating, sleeping and virtually living in this situation until the event is brought to some kind of close.

Once a deadline has been set for a press conference it has to be adhered to. While media contact on a smaller scale is often preferred, a press conference allows you the scope during a crisis of having the media in one place and being able to address them in a planned sequence over a series of hours or days.

Most of the major resource companies and oil companies have permanent corporate media centres with full telecommunication and videoconference facilities. Sometimes the media are ushered into a corporate theatrette and other times media conferences are given in a church hall or a disused shed.

One of the most elaborate media briefing rooms in the world is in Florida at the Kennedy Space Centre. It was set up to handle something like 500 journalists for each space shuttle launch. When the *Challenger* shuttle exploded, many additional newspaper people poured into the NASA Centre to receive news of the horrific disaster. The Centre is equipped with state-of-the-art meeting room equipment including press 'super desks' equipped with individual telephones, power, computer terminals and satellite contact. The room is surrounded with compartments filled with information material and audiovisual support, photographs and research libraries. There is a full catering block providing 24-hour food and drink.

In addition to the fully equipped domed press centre, NASA also has a grandstand, not unlike a sports grandstand, several miles away from the launch area. This is also equipped with full media facilities, telecommunication and co-axial cable links to allow the press satellite contact around the world. In fact, the media grandstand was used during the *Challenger* disaster to handle major press briefings because of the huge number of media present.

A word of warning about the press conference. A poor quality news conference or a cover-up will mean the media will leave and search out better sources for their information.

A press conference has to convey the key information of a crisis to the media, who will communicate that information to its audiences. A good press conference needs to be well-organised ahead of the event and the room should be set up in a theatre style with sufficient seats and work tables.

The presentation end of any press conference room needs to have a lectern and possible facilities for whiteboards and diagrams (see Figure 6.1). The symbol or logo of the company should be highly visable in this area. It should also have an entrance and exit door for the spokesperson, allowing them to enter the room confidently, present their message, take some questions and then leave without having to move through the crowd.

One of the classic examples of how not to do a press conference was shown by a chemical company in Queensland, Australia, that had been through a fairly dramatic environmental problem. The media conference was called and a large media contingent settled into the selected media room, chomping at the bit for answers from the company's spokesperson. He came in from the back of the room and proceeded to the other end of the room, made his statement, answered two questions and then attempted to leave.

Suddenly the enthusiastic brigade of reporters formed a tight front line with cameras and microphones thrust in his face and he could not advance or retreat. There was no exit door and no way out. So he stayed an extra half an hour while he attempted to answer many unplanned questions.

You will notice that President Clinton has an exit door in the White House press room. There are always several FBI agents on hand to add further assistance to a necessary departure.

What are the five things necessary to be prepared before a conference?

1. Prepare news kits
   Make sure they contain your speech and all the information about the topic. Make sure there are enough for all the reporters.
2. Check the area and rehearse
   Well before the conference, walk around the area so you have a feel for it. Rehearse the news conference prior to the event so you have a clear picture of what you are saying and how long it will take.
3. Check the public address system
   Make sure it works and is the right volume to be heard clearly at the back of the room. Do not leave this to the last minute.

*Figure 6.1* The press conference room

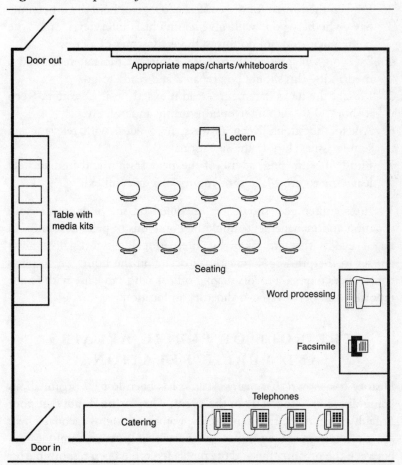

4. Check power for television and radio
   Television requires lights that draw high amperage. Make sure the venue is capable of handling the load.
5. Make sure your website and facsimile facilities are ready to provide additional support.

Now you are ready for your press briefing conference. A veritable mass of journalists are waiting to talk to you. You have a great chance of gaining favourable coverage because you have provided the media with the facilities and the support they need to get the message out. The theatre is ready, the script is prepared and the leading person is about to deliver their lines.

Here is a typical running sheet for a press conference:

1. Welcome the media—this can be done by your public affairs director.
2. Explain the format for the conference—give them the timeframe.
3. Say whether you will give individual interviews after the conference—do not do this in the early stages of a crisis.
4. Say you will present them with copies of the statement and a media kit—this should be prepared and ready to go.
5. Present the news statement—read it exactly as it is written. Keep it short. Deal with interruptions firmly and politely.
6. Ask for questions. Keep answers short—deal with relevant and serious issues. Ignore the sensational.
7. Finish the meeting, advise of the next session and immediately leave the room. Make sure you make a graceful exit.

Press conferences should be scheduled on the hour in a serious situation and management should be conscious of press deadlines. In major events that are taken by international networks, live news crosses to the press conference may occur on the hour. These news conferences require a media staging officer who can liaise with senior reporters and network co-ordinators on location.

# THE ROLE OF PUBLIC AFFAIRS AND PUBLIC RELATIONS

History has shown that many a battle has been lost by organisations being discredited too early in the event. There is no doubt that poor or faulty communication can lose the communications agenda. There are no shortage of examples to show that poor communication between the organisation and the media has often been responsible for misunderstandings, ill will and the creation of rumour and innuendo.

As a prerequisite to any crisis, there have to be totally up-to-date lists available of the main media, the journalists, chiefs-of-staff, editors, reporters and the program producers.

It is important to take into account that every public affairs and public relations professional will have done their best at establishing strong relations with essential media. Judy Smith, White House and NBC communications veteran, cites a perfect example about building the right relationships with the media. She wrote in the *Public Relations Strategist*:

"It is critical to establish relationships with the media prior to the need for emergency contact. Make sure key media contacts have emergency telephone numbers for 24-hour use. And make sure they know who to contact.

"One example—when President George Bush became ill and collapsed during a state dinner hosted by Japanese Prime Minister Kiichi Miyazawa in January 1992, the media immediately started to speculate about Bush's condition. Press Secretary Marlin Fitzwater was getting information from the President's doctor, while I spoke with as many reporters as possible, asking them to hold off on speculation until we had the facts. Although the event, which was televised worldwide, looked severe, we convinced the media that the President was only suffering from a garden variety flu and there was no need for alarm. Having good relationships with the media helped prevent the spread of misinformation, which would have caused unnecessary public concern."

But a word of warning, frequently the media that confront an organisation during a crisis are in a hurry. They are not your day-to-day feature writers or story writers. They are the investigative, front-page journalists who want a story at any cost and are skilled in the art of getting it. These people can only be dealt with by experienced and prepared personnel. These journalists will know in the first few minutes whether the organisation is on top of things or whether they are dealing with amateurs.

The public affairs and public relations role in a crisis can be wrongly positioned like any of the team players in the aforementioned crisis management team. There is many a crisis team that has been 'taken over' by the enthusiastic public relations executive who is keen to lead the media agenda at the cost of failing to communicate with many of the other stakeholders.

There is no doubt that as we move into the new century, concerns about how messages are designed and communicated, and the value of relationships between audiences, will become a priority. The continual evaluation of public attitudes related to how an organisation does business, will be at the centre of most business strategy. We will see more senior public affairs and public relations people working with CEOs and boards to sound the kind of warnings that organisations need when making major decisions that herald change.

In a crisis, the role of the professional communicator is one of the most important, but it must be part of an overall strategy. Setting up systems to monitor the media is essential—locally, nationally and internationally. Much of the work can be done beforehand in terms of setting up these systems to deal with the pressure of media, community and government.

It becomes one of the major tasks of the public affairs or public relations counsel during a crisis to remind management of the attitudes and opinions of the people they are trying to reach. Breaking down the barriers of industry jargon and legal demands is one of the tasks to be confronted. Incidentally, if the key players in the media, the government and the community cannot get through your switchboard or past your mobile telephone for some early answers, then the public affairs and public relations strategy is lost.

## CONTROL POINTS

☐ Do not blame the media. Crises are news and the media needs the facts.

☐ Understand what the media want well before an incident.

☐ A spokesperson should not only be able to speak, but they must be able to understand who their audience is.

☐ Key communication issues in crises are:
- human life;
- the current situation;
- accurate facts and figures; and
- what you are doing to help the problem.

☐ Crisis media training programs must teach agenda control.

☐ In these days of instant news grabs, longwinded statements are useless.

☐ A press conference is an opportunity to deliver one message to a large number of media.

☐ Setting up systems to monitor the media is essential.

# 7

# MANAGING THE
# OVERSEAS CRISIS

The tropical jungle of Kalimantan had been home to the small band of exploratory mining engineers for nearly two years. They had never felt comfortable with the denseness of the jungle or the hot, damp temperatures. But there was some reward in the last few days. They had seen some strong readings for precious metals above the river bed and they were returning back to base with good news. As they moved around the bend in the river, the small boat hit the rocky river bed and immediately sprung a leak. Suddenly three men were in the water, dragging themselves to dry land. Their two-way radio had been lost with the rest of their kit. On the banks of the river now, they were faced with a new drama — a small band of serious looking local people dressed in combat gear and carrying large automatic weapons. The engineers had no plan and no back-up communication technology to call for help. Did the company have a kidnap for ransom plan?

The growing interest in investment abroad means that many of the world's largest companies are continually moving into new areas offering a broad range of opportunities. Growth for US and UK companies in oil, gas, mining and construction continues, as does the development in areas of manufacturing, telecommunication, retail and financial services. The fastest growing new development areas are China, South America and Eastern Europe.

As companies go global, the threat to the security of people, technology, information and assets gains in impact. Doing business in foreign countries does have crisis connotations and can mean a life or death difference for an organisation.

Dealing with the problems of a changing political arena, threats of bribery, sabotage, vandalism, theft, having to deal and negotiate with irrational customers in distant locations, being faced with problems of armed intrusion or trespassers and the growing international problem of drug abuse, are all threats that need to be recognised and planned for.

Coca–Cola, McDonald's and Shell are some of the international brand names that have struck problems operating in new markets. Coca–Cola discovered the intense security issues related to selling their world famous soft drink in a mafia-ridden new Russia. Threats, extortion, hijacks, robbery and violence have all become part of marketing the product in that country. McDonald's too, have had to deal with the Russian way of doing business. But they have also had to handle a far tougher challenge in opening a shopfront in Beijing. They struck a major crisis when their future premises' lease was cancelled and they were virtually out in the street until new central premises could be located.

Most companies live in a society that is generally reasonable and orderly. Our governments, businesses and infrastructure provide a fairly secure situation. This allows business plans to be accomplished at a reasonable level of success. Even planning for crisis can be based on the premise of achieving, in most cases, an effective response and responsible control. Not so in some of the newer growing economies.

Doing business in countries which have an unstable political structure, surrounded by insecurity, greed and often cruelty and violence, devoid of legitimate police forces, does call for a proactive approach to crisis management.

Western governments worldwide have been dealing with the problems of doing business with these countries for years. Consular staff and trade delegations have battled their way through the security problems and set up a network of bureaucratic contacts that work across a broad spectrum of issues. Corporations seldom have this type of support system or this kind of clout.

Hans Koschnick, the German EU (European Union) Administrator, tells an amazing story of fear and fanatics. He sat outside the 'Eru' Hotel in the Herzegovinian city of Mostar in his BMW car while an angry crowd gathered, preventing him from moving into the hotel. The 67-year old politician listened to the screams as the crowd began to move out of control. 'Hang him!' 'Shoot him!' They were all over the car, kicking, bumping, hitting and bashing the windows. Then shots were fired. In fact, seven bullet impact marks were discovered around the car. Fortunately, this was no ordinary car. It was the BMW 750iL security limousine built with maximum protection and mobility, with its own remote control, bulletproof tyres, bulletproof armouring built into the body shell, fresh air systems to prevent gas attacks, an exclusive patented emergency exit system as well as protective glazing tested against pistol and rifle ammunition and high-impact hand-held weapons. After 50 minutes, the police took control and the crowds were gone.

An amazing snapshot of the kind of terrorist attack that can face the high-ranking politician or businessperson or administrator. In this case, planning and technology had saved the day. The internal communication system enabled the driver to call for assistance and in the meantime, the structure of the car gave the very highest lifesaving protection.

Kidnapping and hijacking have seized the international media agenda and terrorism is a persistent threat. Extremists continue their anti-western activities in many of the new economies, and communities are building in strength in their opposition to the nature of foreign investment or environmental damage. Companies operating in other countries are at continual risk from foreign governments involved in political change, domestic terrorism and a wide range of security issues.

It was a shocking experience for a group of tourists travelling through Yemen who faced the horror of seeing some of their travelling companions executed in a shoot-out between Islamic terrorists and Yemenite troops early in 1999.

Three Britons and an Australian died in the shoot-out. The group were touring in Yemen when they were captured by Islamic terrorists. The tourists were given no option but to do the best they could in a situation that they had neither been trained for nor sufficiently warned about. British detectives and FBI officers investigating the killings had to consider the fact that there was a plan by Islamic extremists to target British and US interests in that area. The nature of the ordeal raises questions about the depth of security briefing provided for tourists or, indeed, business people travelling in dangerous or sensitive regions.

Has terrorism increased? Aside from the horrific Oklahoma bombing, the explosion at the World Trade Centre in New York, the attack on the US military in Saudi Arabia and the graphic, televised hostage situation at the Japanese Ambassador's resident in Peru, the FBI have reported that terrorism incidents have declined in the last decade.

The *Risk Management* magazine, July 1997, reports:

There were only two domestic terrorist attacks in 1995, down from 51 in 1992. The CIA reports that international attacks are not only less frequent but have been less lethal than incidents during the 1980s. Explosive devices used in international terrorism are declining. Even more dramatic is the reduction in terrorist and criminal activities directed against civil aviation. According to the American Society for Industrial Security, this dramatic drop can be attributed to several factors: sound government policy, aggressive law enforcement and the break-up of the Soviet Union.

Recognition of the need to deal with crisis on foreign soil has to be at the top of the agenda of any investment opportunity. Early identification of threats or problems related to community hostility, corruption, native title or environmental pressure groups can begin the crisis management planning process.

Building and educating a crisis management team has to be based on the local management possessing an understanding of both internal and external threat perspectives related to the country in which they are operating.

Because of the tyranny of distance and time, any international crisis management plan needs a seamless communication structure so that critical decisions can be made on-the-spot and adequate resources can be committed quickly and efficiently.

In the case of Bhopal, India, for Union Carbide distance itself was a major factor in the disaster. When the deadly methyl isocyanate gas was released and thousands were critically injured and killed, there was no plan, save the most basic emergency response, to deal with the massive local and international implications which would hit Union Carbide in the months and years to follow.

It was 3.00 a.m. on 3 December 1984 and over five tons of this deadly toxic chemical had vaporised into a gas that slowly moved across the city's suburbs. The chemical had leaked from storage containers at the Union Carbide plant and tragically the gas had been inhaled by thousands of victims. It had also been absorbed through the skin. People lay dying and hundreds of thousands of others were staggering from their homes wheezing from the burning poison.

The company of course could never have a crisis plan to deal with such a massive amount of dead and injured. Back at headquarters in the United States, the phones went crazy while management desperately tried to find in-depth information about what had happened and how. They were struggling with information from their office in Bombay, which in turn was relaying information from the Bhopal area.

The first media response was less than 12 hours after the incident had been reported. Faced with massive legal liability, the company CEO, Warren Anderson, wore the responsibility. He then organised a crisis team to move directly into the area to begin investigating the cause of the situation and to start the tragic recovery process in assisting the victims. This was received very positively by the US business press.

The arrival of Warren Anderson, Union Carbide's CEO, at the airport in Bhopal, was a mini crisis in itself. Warren Anderson was met by the police with arrest warrants charging Union Carbide with culpable homicide and causing death by negligence. After a period of detention, Anderson was released under an arrangement between the Indian and US governments and was immediately flown out of the country. The company's crisis investigation team had moved into the area with a team of scientists to further the investigation.

Operating in other countries can also be a crisis when your own government pulls the plug on your support system. This can be the refusal of political back-up, security support or funding.

## COKE'S HEALTH SCARE

In an international crisis situation where a major high-profile brand is concerned, getting on top of the marketing dimension is one issue that can require resolute actions across many borders.

In June 1999, Coca–Cola, the largest soft drink producer in the world with sales of its product in more than 160 countries, had to deal with the biggest recall in its history when the governments of France, Belgium, Luxembourg and the Netherlands ordered Coca–Cola to remove its products from shelves in stores throughout their countries following a contamination scare.

The contamination scare began in Belgium when more than 100 people were reported ill after consuming the company's soft drinks. After the initial reports, Belgium ordered all Coca–Cola products to be pulled from shop shelves while the problem was investigated. It was joined by Luxembourg, while France imposed partial restrictions, telling Coca–Cola to stop shipping cans and bottles from a plant in

Dunkirk, near the Belgium border, where some of the contaminated products originated. The Netherlands similarly banned all Coke products coming from Belgium.

The company itself went into voluntary recall, withdrawing products from the Dutch market made at a second suspect plant in Antwerp, Belgium. A day later, the scare spread to France when more than 80 people were reported with similar cases of illness, just as officials from the Atlanta-based firm tried to persuade authorities to lift bans on its products imposed in the wake of the first reported illnesses in Belgium.

According to a Reuters News report, Coca–Cola had initially claimed to have traced the origin of the problem to poor carbon dioxide used in bottled drinks made in Antwerp and, in Dunkirk, to a fungicide which had coated the surface of cans. A spokesperson from the Dunkirk plant was reported as saying that the Dunkirk plant had cut production of carbonated beverages by 75 per cent at that time.

But in a telephone interview to Reuters, a company spokesperson was reported as saying that further investigations by Coca–Cola 'had found no health concerns behind the off tastes and smells, which would be enough to cause symptoms such as vomiting and stomach cramps suffered by Belgian teenagers and adults after drinking Coke beverages'.[1]

In a statement reported in *The New York Times*, Coca–Cola confirmed that there had been two problems leading to the recall. The first was that the soft drinks concerned had been bottled using carbon dioxide that was defective. This had caused 'an off taste in the bottled product'. The company said all bottles produced with the defective carbon dioxide, which creates the bubbles in a carbonated soft drink, had been recalled. But it added that the defect affected the taste of the soft drinks only and that the products were safe to drink.

The second problem affected cans of Coke. The cans smelled bad on the outside, and people who opened them and drank the contents became ill. Coca–Cola reportedly claimed that the contents of the can was not affected, but there was a 'package integrity issue'. Again, the Coca–Cola statement said the products were safe.[2]

While the spokesperson claimed that the test results were well received by the ministry, the Health Minister himself said that he was not pleased with Coca–Cola's handling of the problem, and was particularly irritated that the company's communications with health authorities had occurred through news conferences. The massive recall that led to several countries banning Coca–Cola, was a blow to an organisation that prides itself on quality standards and control. While the recall affected less than 1 per cent of Coca–Cola's global sales, it still came at a time when one of the Atlanta-based Coca–Cola companies was making a bid for Coca–Cola Beverages, the European distributor of the product.

Importantly, this product recall was a spokesperson's nightmare in terms of managing reponses on many fronts. The company had to deal with a number of European governments and their health ministries, and the European Union itself. It was dealing with a demanding media on many fronts throughout Europe and, particularly, in the United States and London. Beseiged by comments from a broad range of observers, including academics, government officials, competitors and consumers, Coca–Cola's plan in response to this particular crisis had to address the concerns of a huge number of stakeholders. Coca–Cola chairman and CEO flew to Europe to apologise personally to people affected.

1   Focus–Belgium reviews Coke drink ban', *Reuters News*, 16 June 1999.
2   Reported in 'Coke recalled in European health scare', *Australian Financial Review*, 17 June 1999.

# EVACUATION—IN THE HEAT OF THE BATTLE

The worst nightmare for a company is knowing that its people and assets are under siege in another country. And as anyone who has been in this situation can attest, in the midst of a rising incident, it is the most emotional time for individuals and their family at the location.

Just in this decade, we have seen hundreds of thousands of people evacuated from countries such as the Philippines, Indonesia, Kuwait, New Guinea, Fiji, and Bosnia. All these evacuations have come at a high emotional and stressful cost to organisations and individuals.

When a disaster involving military action strikes, the last thing you need to do is waste valuable time fumbling through files to find out what has to be done. Every organisation doing business in another country needs a custom-tailored alternative evacuation solution. This is a time where the crisis management and recovery planning process is triggered by an in-country evacuation.

Basically, it is a people project. It requires getting management to envisage the worst possible event that may turn their lives upside down and make them plan ahead. This kind of planning cannot be done on-the-spot because of the required interface with embassies, consular personnel and security structures in that country.

The purpose of the evacuation and contingency plan is to minimise the impact of unfavourable events regardless of their magnitude. There are some horror stories of people being caught at airports for days, waiting for flights out of countries where airports eventually are closed. There are tales of people losing passports or being unable to find sufficient cash to provide the necessary bribe or enticement to officials. There are tragic stories of families being separated by significant military action that cuts off one side of a city and leaves family members stranded.

A country going through major civil commotion is not only a terrifying experience but an uncertain situation where even the most experienced personnel can be caught up in a web of unlikely events. An early warning system is essential and is a starting point to the ultimate plan. Certainly, every contingency plan has, at its heart, the safety of people, but at the same time a major portion of the plan needs to involve the recovery of assets and the continuation of business in that country.

## LINKING THE PARENT COMPANY

Ironically, some of the methods of doing business in foreign countries that are designed to save money can actually put an organisation's whole presence in that country at threat. For example, setting up a plant in an area where labour is plentiful but transport is difficult, can put security pressures on executive staff who are managing the project. They can be in danger from local criminal and political instability or their families can be at risk from the problems they may face travelling on dangerous roads.

The key to crisis management in a foreign business environment is a plan that adds local knowledge and expertise to help manage the threats. Coming to terms with the most efficient response to a crisis or emergency will depend, to a great extent, on the reliability of the planning and preparation that takes place beforehand.

In a recent experience in an Asian country going through severe political change and instability, a large transport company had attempted to set up an emergency evacuation structure for their people. They were working to deal with the threat of terrorism or the possibility of politically motivated kidnapping. In certain parts of South America and Asia, there is a continuous problem with short-term kidnapping for political or criminal purposes. In some Asian countries, there is rarely a day that goes by where there is not some reference to a financial deal done with terrorists related to a kidnap situation.

116

The company was slow in putting together guidelines for protecting the organisation against potential problems. A number of employees at the company then decided to formulate a plan themselves. They decided that if their families were the victims of kidnap for ransom or any form of terrorism, they would create their own group of negotiators and deal directly with the kidnappers.

Their fear was exacerbated by an incident where the wife of one of the employees was threatened by a chauffeur driving their children to school. She fortunately was able to take control of the vehicle and drive her family to a safe situation. Her husband, with other expatriate friends, formed a local response group to deal with the situation, which led to a violent retaliation that involved company, government, police and consular officials. The situation did get out of control and the company was the loser. If there had been a plan there in the first place, the security threat would have been easier to deflect.

In this case, management stepped in and set up a formal crisis management plan that prescribed a security policy and offered guidance to ensure a state of pre-emergency readiness.

They worked with a private international security company to reduce the risks through a security program that identified the company's exposures to problems in that region. Greater intelligence was gathered to ensure an understanding of the threats and appropriate measures were taken to protect the management, staff and their families, but also to ensure continued operations.

## GUIDELINES FOR INTERNATIONAL OFFICE OR SITE PLANS

A crisis in another country often does not fit into any known framework. The organisational response, therefore, has to deal with the problem of finding people to manage the problem at the same time as anticipating the escalation factor and providing support for the most exposed aspects of the business. There is simply little time for planning, organising, equipping or training once the crisis is imminent.

Importantly, the crisis management approach needs to ensure that the various operations and projects of an international operation are in a constant state of readiness and that crisis teams know what to do and how to do it.

Basically, the objectives of any plan should be to protect the company's people and assets.

International operations crisis management objectives should:

- protect the life of employees and their families;
- protect assets and earnings by restoring normal operations rapidly;
- protect the local community and environment;
- minimise damage to corporate reputation; and
- retain effective relationships with government of the country.

Because international business management and employees could be cut off for long periods from the parent company by failure of communication lines, it is important that teams are trained in advance to follow prescribed guidelines in their crisis response. The way in which the crisis is tackled will depend on the quality of training and briefing for the crisis teams before the event.

The plan needs to clearly establish authority and responsibilities at every level. It is useful here to define mobilisation actions and list contact points with details about communication links and notification procedures.

Interfacing with external agencies is a valuable part of crisis planning in other countries because the crisis management response may well include support systems from embassies or law enforcement agencies. Setting these communication links up in advance is vital to the success of the plan.

The plan should contain details of the team roles and responsibilities, setting out the core action group at each location who are responsible for managing the problem. It will be their responsibility to assess the situation and respond accordingly with the necessary resources required. They will also need to contact and communicate with other teams in the region and the necessary stakeholders affected, including head office in the home country.

In some cases, the crisis management team may only be one or two people. This is particularly the case for exploration, research or transport teams working in distant locations. It is still important that these small teams have an understanding of how to pinpoint a crisis and what on-the-spot actions they have to achieve to protect life and ongoing operations.

## THE THREAT DIFFERENTIAL

Threat and risk identification changes more rapidly as a business operates internationally. As a company sends more of their personnel abroad to manage global markets, so the security threats as well as business threats, widen. Continual struggles for nationalist, religious and ethnic identities have significantly increased the risk of political problems and this requires continual monitoring.

Some companies work with international security organisations to monitor security issues in overseas countries and to maintain a watch on evacuation readiness. Many of these companies can provide emergency assistance in the event of civil or political unrest. Some even provide specialist services in hostage negotiation and security-supported evacuation.

The fact is, as the threats change, so they need to be prepared for. Assessing the threat and its response is a priority.

It depends entirely on the kind of business you do and where you do it and, to some extent, how you do it, that predicts the threats that may need to be considered in the dynamics of your crisis response.

For Pan Am in 1988, it was the explosion on Flight 103 from Heathrow, over Lockerbie, Scotland, that shattered the night and shed masses of debris and bodies over hundreds of miles of countryside starting fires and damaging buildings.

Pan Am offices worldwide were thrown into chaos and Pan Am business was seriously affected. The terrorist act was given enormous publicity related to airport and air cargo security. Pan Am, as any airline in that situation, had to deal with a crisis in another country— fortunately a friendly country.

While their response was efficient in terms of dealing with the emergency in another country, there was considerable criticism about the fact that the Chairman of Pan Am did not visit the site. When the Lauda Air 767 crashed in Thailand in 1991, Nicki Lauda travelled to the site and spent many days dealing with the emotional issues related to passenger deaths.

More recently, Pan Am has ceased operations as one of America's formerly great airlines and Lockerbie remains a turning point in increased provision of security to safeguard passengers and crew members internationally.

There is no doubt that damage can be minimised to overseas offices if those offices take their threat identification seriously and review what things could go wrong.

Some of the most common crisis threats at overseas locations are:

- disruption to operations
- change of government attitude or policy
- industrial action
- economic collapse and devaluation
- lawlessness and hostile demonstration
- transport accident

- fatality
- fire or explosion
- environmental damage
- serious bad weather (hurricane, cyclone, flood, tidal wave, fire storm)
- medical emergency
- epidemic.

Less common threats, but those that might affect the short- and long-term prospects of the company, are:

- terrorist activities
- sabotage of plant and operations
- kidnap for ransom
- violent assault
- confinement or imprisonment of employees and families
- extortion
- contamination of product
- drug trafficking
- murder of expatriates
- cessation of commercial international flights.

You cannot have a plan for every crisis. You cannot create a plan for every threat. But preparing a set of basic plans to deal with the most likely problems gives you a chance to get ahead of the problem. Having the decision-making checklists to make sure you have covered all the things that have to be done could save lives.

## EVACUATION PLANNING

For organisations with offices in other countries, when systems begin to break down during political change or military problems, there has to be a plan to manage not just the crisis surrounding business continuity, but also the crisis related to evacuation of employees and their families.

In Indonesia, foreign nationals went through some emotionally difficult times as tanks rolled in to defend the city of Jakarta in 1998. In one particular case, a group of expatriate women had moved to rescue their children from schools on one side of Jakarta. As the rioting escalated, the mothers and their children huddled together overnight and eventually escaped in darkness in a convoy of cars pushing over the barriers on the toll road.

Main access roads had been cut off by looters and mobs and life was made very difficult as company executives and staff waited in other parts of Jakarta to hear news of their families. The American, British and Singapore embassies gave instructions to their citizens to keep off the streets, while other embassies were recommending stocking up with food and essential needs. Some embassies had already suggested their citizens should evacuate the country.

When things go wrong, it may well be time to get out. How to get out without risking the lives of employees, losing assets and earnings, and inevitably destroying your reputation, is a problem that has to be managed with precise guidelines and tested.

Crisis evacuation plans are a priority to any organisation working overseas and should be prepared with the assistance of a professional security or experienced emergency planning expert. An evacuation team needs to be formed to cover responsibilities such as human resources, security, families, victims, commercial and financial issues and administration.

The essential factor in evacuation planning is to prevent chaos. Well in advance, decision-making tools and checklists need to be created to provide managers with action plans to respond to exceptional circumstances.

Threats need to be placed in a severity matrix with trigger points that activate a state of readiness or specifically required actions to depart. These trigger points should relate to the evacuation planning process for expatriates put in place by your organisation's embassy in the country concerned.

In most cases, it is recommended that company evacuation plans are co-ordinated with embassy evacuation plans. However, many corporate organisations prefer to have an earlier state of readiness and departure for families and employees than the recommended embassy standard, particularly if their company or organisation has a somewhat sensitive relationship in that country of operation.

The ultimate approval authority for evacuation needs to be given by either the chief executive in the country concerned or the site or location manager in that country. Depending on the circumstances, the evacuations may involve dependents' children first, followed by other family and finally actual employees. At all times, the evacuation may be ordered by either the embassy or the company with little or no advance warning.

It also needs to be assumed that evacuation by the normal means of transport may not be possible and alternative evacuation may be required. Airports may be closed and evacuation by land or sea may well be necessary.

## Planning assumptions

What planning assumptions need to be considered in a structured evacuation plan to move people and belongings out of a city or country at a critical time?

- Decide on evacuation team and leadership for decision.
- Identify key threat trigger points. Prepare a severity matrix related to embassy plan.
- Decide on mobilisation phases and evacuation levels.
- Confirm designated location for control centre with sufficient communication technolog. Alternative location should be identified.
- Confirm safe havens and reception areas where personnel and families can wait until safe travel is confirmed for departure.
- Confirm registration of all personnel and families with embassies.
- Set up regular intelligence monitor to ensure assessment of situation from embassies, government agencies, security organisations, field staff, customers, contractors, joint venture partners, etc.
- Communication and technology need to be clearly identified ahead of time and tested. Mobile and cellular telephones and two-way radio back-up must be confirmed.
- Sufficient medical support needs to be located to provide first-aid or deal with pre-existing medical conditions.
- Security for dealing with both the safety of people and documents and records needs to be identified. This should be co-ordinated internally and supported by approved outside professional personnel.
- Travel and transport—expatriate employees and their families need to be issued with sufficient air and land transport tickets (pre-purchased) plus cash advances for each family member. Limits should be set on accommodation and food costs. Preferred charter options with details of flight clearances through customs, immigration and security controls at alternative airports should be identified. Drivers and chauffeurs should be security checked and rehearsed.
- A spokesperson needs to be appointed to communicate messages with all key stakeholders, including the media.
- Evacuation plans need to be co-ordinated with all foreign and local schools where expatriate employees' children are in attendance. Communication lines should be clearly established between the school and the families and company.
- Route maps should be distributed to all expatriate employees to identify destinations and departure points.

- Personnel and families should review their personal stockpile of food, water and fuel.
- Security of documents and the availability of shredding equipment should be confirmed.
- Accommodation on arrival at evacuation destination needs to be arranged in advance with the necessary support systems for food, drink, medical and counselling.
- Special facilities need to be considered for evacuation of dead and injured personnel with specific requirements for transport on arrival at destination and dealing with victims' families.

## KIDNAP FOR RANSOM

Kidnap for ransom, confinement or imprisonment of employees or families is a threat that has to be dealt with in a most sensitive and precise manner. Today, senior management of businesses and institutions must have a policy in place that provides the facilities and resources to deal effectively with a potential kidnap issue. Prevention of course is better than cure. The more trained managers are in dealing with the situation, the better.

Whether it be a politically motivated kidnapping or a criminal ransom, the fact is it has to be dealt with rapidly with the greatest of care taken for the victim or victims.

Most countries have strict laws that prohibit this act. The problem of dealing with ransom payments, however, is not under any international agreement. It is therefore important to develop a mechanism to make sure that victims and their families and other affected employees are protected to the highest degree.

Kidnapping and hijacking have grabbed the world's attention. There are countless examples of how terrorists have exploited and manipulated people and governments through the media in an effort to terrorise populations and gain support for their cause.

It is therefore important that any planning process to deal with kidnap threats or security is done so with the assistance of qualified professional advisers. Particularly the area of sensitive negotiations with perpetrators should be handled by qualified negotiators, with pre-arranged agreements as to the process of dealing with the situation.

Because dealing with local law enforcement agencies may hinder the process in some countries, prior arrangements need to be made with federal law enforcement offices in the home country or with security advisers at the local embassy or consulate.

It is important that kidnap plans and particular information related to sensitive financial arrangements be given the highest security status. Many senior police officers have the view that no financial structure should be published related to ransom payments.

Response strategies should address the following nine issues:

1.  Corporate policy on dealing with a kidnap situation
    This needs to be stated well in advance. The CEO and the board of the organisation need to confirm details of who negotiates on behalf of a kidnap victim. Decisions have to be made about ransom payments (illegal in many countries). Prior approval of the use of outside consultants and their formal role in the process needs to be arranged.

2.  Arrangements with law enforcement agencies
    Most major companies and organisations, through their security management, spend time being briefed by national and international law enforcement agencies regarding hostage or kidnap for ransom situations.

    Prior advice from senior government security officials and police is useful in the planning process, however in some countries, this liaison should be handled with sensitivity.

3.  Corporate security consultants' support
    There are experts in the field of security and kidnap events. When an issue such as this strikes, it is useful to have a professional organisation to call on for intelligence and response advice. This needs to be arranged in advance so that the process for dealing with a security emergency can be pre-planned and rehearsed.

    The choice of outside consultants should be based on their training and capability in the field and their comprehensive network of professional assistance available at the location of the incident.

4.  Administration team roles and responsibilities
    Security issues that involve a kidnap for ransom or hostage situation can take days to resolve. This usually results in the disruption of senior management ranks, both in the country of the event and at head office. It is therefore useful to identify the CORE management team required for various actions for dealing with the situation. It is also important to understand who carries the authority to make major decisions at any time of the day or night.

5.  Communication and care of victims' family
    This is a highly emotional time for families of victims. They will

require assistance wherever they are but particularly if they are not in the country where the event has taken place. They will certainly require a continual update of the situation. They may well require counselling from experienced psychologists.

They will require assistance in dealing with the release of private information related to their partner or spouse. They may require transport to the country concerned. They will have to be briefed on dealing with foreign governments and the media.

6.  Security compliance
    There are security issues related to most kidnap situations. Personal security may need to be arranged immediately for other executives or managers and their families in the region concerned. Additional security may be required for offices, buildings and houses. Transport routes may need to be changed or altered. Private security companies and law enforcement agencies can assist with this process.

7.  Media management and message strategy
    An act of terrorism relies on achieving propaganda goals. Many kidnap situations are performed to manipulate the media and the government of the country concerned. In a serious security situation, the media has to be very tightly controlled. Misinformation or rumour and innuendo can lead to a critical outcome.

    The media has to be part of a well-oiled process to control and run the message agenda and achieve compliance of demands. Actions must be strong and clear. It is one time where media co-operation is essential.

    Most law enforcement agencies in Western countries have excellent co-operation from the media in these situations, however, in some parts of the world, this co-operation is unachievable.

8.  Rescue response co-ordination
    Rescue and evacuation need to be linked to the kidnap plan. Resources need to be identified in advance in the areas of aviation, land or sea to provide retrieval and repatriation services. Possibly the most important aspect of rescue response co-ordination is the appointment of a reliable source of transport. This supplier needs to have the capability to arrange transport from high security situations with the necessary back-up of medical teams and equipment. Clearance through customs and government agencies at airports will be an essential part of the requirement.

9. Counselling of victims

Every international business traveller should at some time be given a thorough security briefing on the problems of travel. In some cases, where travellers are moving through high risk countries or zones, they should be given survival courses on coping with capture, robbery and kidnap. Importantly, if they are the victims of a serious incident, they will suffer serious emotional trauma and will certainly have to deal with a long period of stressful discussions, investigations and interviews. Organisations must provide short- and long-term counselling and security for these people. Re-adjustment to a normal situation will take time and care. The more that is done in the planning to deal with these situations, the more smoothly the recovery process will occur.

Because kidnap for ransom situations requires decisions of great consequence to be made on-the-spot under exceptional circumstances, it is crucial that expert assistance be gained in protecting the victim. Guidelines for dealing with any potentially critical situations can assist managers in the early stages of the event, however professional assistance from an experienced negotiator is essential.

## EVACUATION MEDIA CONTROL

In most major emergency events in foreign countries, local and international media are in search of stories as the event escalates. Stories of people and organisations moving out of disaster situations make essential news and the people involved are central to the story. In an emergency situation, an organisation and its people can be a media target. It is important to take the communications initiative and stay in control of your evacuation plan and not be led by reporters looking for sensational information.

### Reporting relationships

The emergency communication chain of command for media response needs to be clearly defined. This works best when there are pre-established clear lines of emergency communication between the company in a country and its other operations in that country. The same applies to clear lines of emergency communication with the company's head office.

The reporting relationships may be temporary and only relate to the evacuation situation, but each location needs a clear indication of what has been said and by whom.

Ideally, there should be one company media centre in the country where the emergency has occurred. This media centre should be linked for information with the other company locations in that country.

At the same time, this media centre needs to be linked with head office and the nearest related country to the evacuees. The media centre should provide the key spokesperson for the company.

## Spokesperson's specific responsibilities

The principal spokesperson for the company in any emergency situation should be identified in advance, along with the establishment of a media control centre. Remote locations need to link their communications plan with the media control centre.

One spokesperson can deliver one clear message. All personnel should direct their enquiries on the situation to this central spokesperson. Provision also needs to be made for alternatives who will be authorised to speak for the organisation if the designated spokesperson is not available.

The designated spokesperson needs to be advised by the media centre of the organisation's position at all levels of the emergency in order for their responses to reflect the direction of the company.

## Statement of responsibility

What should you say? What do you do when a news crew approaches you to talk on behalf of your experience, to speak on behalf of your company or your country? The important thing to remember is that a refusal to comment or a genuine lack of response to questions is not a crime. In fact, keeping a low profile in this situation is recommended.

Three messages should underline the initial communications effort:

1. 'We do not have a comment on the present situation here. We have taken charge of our particular responsibilities in terms of the safety of our people and have moved to secure their safe departure.'
2. 'Everything is being done to acquire information about our future here. Our emergency plans are being enacted and they provide for a safe and orderly departure of our people.'
3. 'We are confident everyone is safe. The local management of the company have taken charge of all aspects of the business here. As far as we can see at this stage, the business will continue to operate as usual. We have no comment on the political situation here.'

This message strategy requires some skill, especially in the areas of dealing with inquiring journalists, but to be in control of your particular situation is more important than being a commentator for your country.

## Demands on company for statement

In times of emergency situations, large companies are sought after for media comment, i.e. 'International transport giant, "Transporter", have a large involvement in this country and I have with me a spokesperson from that company—are things going to get worse here? Are you worried about your future in this country? Would you like to tell us what you have seen on your way here? Your company has operations deep in the centre of the problem area—is the situation escalating? What do you think about the political problems? Who is responsible?' It is vital to avoid being drawn into a litany of personal opinions and views that may become international news in this situation. What the situation requires is the standard responses as suggested above and/or one of the following:

1. 'We are treating this situation as serious and are taking the best possible response to the situation to assure the safety of our people.'

2. 'I am unable to comment on the situation here and you would be best advised to talk to representatives from the Embassy.'

3. 'Everything is being done to secure the safety of our people. When we have collected more information, we will pass it on to you.'

4. 'It is impossible for me to answer questions about this situation. I do not have sufficient information at this stage. This is really a matter for the Embassy and I know the government has a spokesperson in charge of this area.'

## Statements on injured or missing persons

In the case of a scenario where company people are missing or may be seriously injured in an emergency situation, again it is important to take the communications initiative.

You need to tell it all as you know it and let people know how the company is assisting authorities. At all times, it is important to emphasise how the emergency plans are being enacted and how they work. For example, consider the following responses:

1. 'We are doing everything we can to help these people. It is important to know that there are rescue/medical support systems of the highest standard being mobilised to provide assistance.'

2. 'To the families of these people, I want them to know that everything is being done to give our people concerned the best possible rescue/medical assistance. Emergency plans are being enacted and more information will be provided as soon as possible.'

3. 'We are working with the Embassy, who are in turn negotiating/working with this country's government at the highest possible level to ensure the safety and welfare of our people.'

4. 'We have strong local management in charge of the situation. They are working with their government to secure the safety of our people. Information is being actively sought out, aimed at assisting our people quickly and concisely. We will continue to receive reports here and keep families in touch with the situation as often as possible.'

## Dealing with media conferences (following evacuation)

A media conference may be called in the airport lounge or company office at the first destination after the evacuation. The media conference may well be targeted specifically at the success or failure of the emergency and may demand disclosure of a wide area of information. The conference could well be organised by rescue organisations, media groups or other governments.

A basic policy regarding media conference disclosures needs to be established up-front. The procedure for dealing with these media conferences should be based on a planned message strategy as part of a statement read by the spokesperson.

## The media conference plan

A plan for a media conference should incorporate the following:

- a spokesperson should work with government and public relations representatives;
- prepare an agreed statement;
- make sure the conference area is secure and your exits clear;
- enlist security and advisers;
- during conference, first read the agreed statement;
- offer copies of statement;
- then answer only the questions related to the agreed position;
- speak of planning and response to safety of people;
- speak of support from governments, organisations and technology;
- speak of continual updates and communication;
- move the questions around the room;

- do not respond to sensational or rumour-based questions;
- keep the conference brief and to the point;
- conduct only short, precise interviews afterwards; and
- keep a record of the questions and media personnel attending.

---

# CONTROL POINTS

☐ Doing business in countries with an unstable political structure calls for proactive crisis management.

☐ The tyranny of distance and time requires seamless communication structures for critical decisions.

☐ Consider your government pulling the plug on your support system. Issues like political back-up, security support or funding can be critical.

☐ Kidnap for ransom, confinement or imprisonment of employees or families must be dealt with in the most sensitive and precise manner. Use professional advisors.

☐ Regular intelligence monitors need to be in place to ensure assessment of developing problems.

☐ Crisis evacuation plans should be prepared with the assistance of professional security or experienced emergency planning experts.

☐ Evacuation by normal means of transport may not be possible. Alternative routes need to be identified and evacuation rehearsed.

☐ Evacuation plans need to be co-ordinated with foreign and local schools, where expatriate employees' children are in attendance.

☐ Crisis events in foreign countries may well attract international media and require the organisation to set up a media command post in or near that country.

☐ Prior advice from senior government security officials and police is useful in the planning process, however in some countries, this liaison should be handled with sensitivity.

---

# 8

# RECOVERY PLANNING

The damage was done. The leak of toxic chemicals into the
town's lake had done its worst. Thousands of native birds lay
dead. Plant life around the once green and lively shoreline was
now a brown and grey mass of twisted branches and dead
undergrowth. The civic area, once proudly encouraging families
to bring their barbeques to the water's edge and breathe in the
rich, rare oxygen-laden air, now lay deserted and bare. This
environmental disaster had hit the town between the eyes. The
factory that once proudly carried its corporate symbol high on
the agenda of so many local events was now frowned on. There
was a massive recovery effort required to rebuild the fragile
ecology of the area and regain the confidence of the townspeople.

---

Organisations working in today's competitive and complex
working environment are driving the customer service factor to
win. Keeping up the pace of customer service and brand recognition
are amongst the top priorities of winning. In the case of fast food
chains, it has become their only product differential. It can be said that
consistency of customer service drives most businesses today. It is easy
to understand, therefore, that an organisation cannot afford to lose
time in recovering from a crisis. Even if a business has efficient crisis
plans in place, rapid recovery following a crisis is crucial. Recovery
must be part of the crisis plan.

Recovery means keeping the business going. The worst kind of
event can wipe out a plant, destroy vital information and virtually stop
production, but it should not finish the business. The minute a crisis

is declared, the recovery phase runs parallel. Alternative means of operation have to be put into action, customers need to be advised, suppliers need to be contacted, and employees have to be brought into the picture. Assets and earnings have to be secured and brand reputation and corporate image need to be stabilised.

Insurance recovers and replaces technology and equipment, but the loss of vital facts and figures, the opportunities for competitors to make their mark, and the overall fall in public confidence, can be serious.

The transport industry places recovery and damage control high on their crisis management agenda. Transport disasters have been the death knell of some transport companies. But the only industry to actually die in this century because of disasters is the airship industry. In fact, there were only two disasters—the airship R101 and the *Hindenberg*. And in real numbers there was a combined death toll of less than 100. Small numbers compared to the 1403 lives lost on the *Titanic* or the 230 lives lost on the TWA air disaster in the United States.

In October 1930, the R101 left its mast in Bedfordshire in the United Kingdom with 54 people aboard, loaded to the hilt. The fittings on the airship included silver cutlery, potted palms and heavy Axminster carpeting. There were large supplies of the finest gourmet food and wine with plans for a banquet over Egypt. It was also carrying more diesel oil than was needed.

The airport of Le Bourget in France gave confirmation that the airship was one kilometre north of Beauvais. Then came the report that the R101 had caught fire after not clearing a hill. There were reports of a huge fire in the air and the sound of an explosion as the airship hit the ground and broke up. The cause was never really clarified but it rapidly brought Britain's airship industry to a close.

Germany persisted with airships, particularly with the outstanding *Hindenberg*, the ultimate passenger experience. Magnificently prepared cabins, plush dining room, a library and even a smoking area. This airship made flights to the United States and passengers relied on this as a regular form of transportation.

On 3 May 1937, the *Hindenberg* flew into her American landing area from Germany. Families of passengers awaited at the Lakehurst Terminus. The media were there. A radio reporter, with his wire recorder, had decided that this was an interesting event to review. He moved through the landing processes as the airship slowly lowered its bulk to the ground from the mooring mast. Then, without any warning, there was a flash. In the midst of this broadcast, the man, engulfed in emotion, screamed 'it's flashing, flashing, flashing terribly,

132

it's bursting into flames'. This historical and frightening broadcast was one of the first on-the-spot broadcasts of an actual disaster in action. The crew of the *Hindenberg* did an outstanding job of helping injured passengers and crew from the burning inferno. Thirty-six people out of the 97 passangers died.

This was the end of the airship industry. The media gave the disaster worldwide headlines and the broadcast was aired on radio stations internationally. Public outcry and fear was enormous.

The industry reviewed its options but recovery was not one of them. Safety and lack of capability signed the death warrant. The Germans removed other airships from their fleet and both the United Kingdom and Germany closed their factories and hangars. It was all over.

One wonders how much *risk* figured in the departure of that industry. In those days, was there sufficient time given for realistic evaluation of the risks versus the benefits of new innovation?

## RISK AND RECOVERY

As any good risk manager will tell you, effective risk management involves clear risk or threat identification, then estimation and evaluation of the magnitude of its effect so you can control or manage the problem.

One important aspect of risk management is understanding the effect a threat can have on an organisation and how quickly that organisation can recover from the effect of that threat. Risk management is very much asset driven, where crisis management is more stakeholder driven. Crisis threats tend to be broader and deeper and their effect can destabilise a company's well-being. Once the threat has been realised, it can be mitigated against by recovery planning.

Recovery planning should start long before a crisis happens. Organisations generally prepare for crises by reviewing their threats and risks, implementing back-up support systems and preparing a range of responses to deal with the situation. But it is the post-crisis issues that are very often forgotten. The right preparation can minimise post-crisis costs, prevent legal compensation and lead to a much easier recovery.

On 18 July 1984, a gunman entered a McDonald's restaurant in San Ysidro, California and shot 40 people with his M16 rifle. In an act of total madness, James Huberty killed 21 and seriously injured 19 people. A SWAT team sniper from the San Diego police force finally brought Huberty down with a deadly accurate shot.

For McDonald's Restaurants, this was the last possible thought in their minds. A berserk gunman running rampage in their rush hour. They had no plan for this shocking act. The headlines rang loud and clear—'Big Mac Attack' and 'McDonald's Massacre'.

Right from the start, McDonald's were hit hard by the publicity. They were popular and this kind of violation became a possibility in any McDonald's restaurant. Tragic pictures of children and families as victims of the shooting made the front pages of nearly every newspaper in the United States. Fear of copycat killings lingered in the background.

McDonald's response was rapid. They moved quickly to provide physical and emotional support to the families of the dead and injured. They paid hospital bills and flew in next of kin and also provided counselling, wherever possible. They took the risk of being accused of being responsible for this incident but quickly the public came out in support of their efforts to try every conceivable way to help those affected. They gained the respect of a highly concerned and affected public.

A survivor's fund was begun by Joan Kroc, the widow of McDonald's founder, Ray Kroc, who was deeply upset by the tragedy. She made a contribution of US$100,000 to begin the fund and this attracted enormous support. The McDonald's company followed this with a further US$1 million. The site of the shocking disaster was closed permanently and it was decided not to sell the property but to level it and to hand the property over to the community. A new McDonald's was opened at another site some three blocks away.

Recovery had become part of McDonald's crisis management response. There had been massive loss of life, sales took a long time to recover, but the business continued. Their recovery had encompassed every type of member of the community from the victims, the families, the emergency workers, the neighbours and most of all, the families who were customers of McDonald's.

Any worthwhile recovery plan will normally uncover a number of unsuspected areas of vulnerability, and will be a valuable process whether or not a crisis hits. For instance the development of superior maintenance programs, increased security measures, enhanced accounting systems, and improved internal procedures and communication processes. It will also assist in overcoming more easily many of the regular, smaller, but irritating business interruptions

Preparing a tailored recovery plan will, therefore, necessitate a team approach. Workshop sessions should involve senior executives, line managers and individual employees to ensure the recovery plan can be drilled down through the organisation to cover all contingencies and facilities, and to allocate responsibilities in a crisis. Like any other component of the overall crisis management plan, the recovery plan should be regularly tested and reviewed to retain its robustness and integrity.

## RETURNING TO NORMAL

The preparation of a crisis recovery plan gives management the opportunity to eliminate or minimise potential problems which could continue to disrupt company operations. At the same time, it can identify ahead of time any alternative means of operations and provide rapid and smooth restoration of service.

A proactive plan for operational recovery needs to be set up under the following headings:

- identification of the most likely crisis scenarios and their impact as shown on the threat list; and
- analysis of relevant scenarios in terms of goals for recovery, short- and long-term strategies to achieve those goals, and critical path.

## ASSET AND EARNING REPLACEMENT

In the case of asset replacement, the first action is to consider the damage to any given asset by the threat identified. The recovery goal will then be to replace that asset by a certain date and within a given timescale.

To achieve this goal, any recovery strategy will need a number of key elements, such as a description of the replacement asset, supplier details, lead times, a methodology for demolition or removal of the damaged asset, and a critical path for the construction of the replacement asset.

If the damaged asset will result in a loss of sales, it will be necessary to identify how you can maintain some sales during the period of interruption, how to create a strategy for maintaining customer relationships.

## THE INTERNAL EFFECT

Australia's largest department store had invested in a stylish fashion presentation featuring Australia's internationally famous model, business woman and film star—Elle Macpherson. She came to a Myer

Grace Bros store in Adelaide and attracted a huge audience of fashion conscious women and a somewhat smaller audience of enthusiastic young men. The fashion show featured some of the most scant but exciting underwear ever featured on a public catwalk and the audience appeared to love it. The response for a short time became almost uncontrollable and some of the management of the store became concerned with the crowd control.

But it was after the fashion parade that the crisis occurred. One of the audience, a young man, evidently became so emotionally disturbed at the event that he apparently took his life. The effect on the people of Adelaide, the customers of the store and the employees was devastating. Certainly the effect on Elle was clear—she gave an emotional response through the media to this event.

Myer Grace Bros did everything they could. They handled hundreds of inquiries from the media throughout Australia and worldwide. They counselled their staff and reviewed their approach to instore events and crowd control. Recovery from a sales point of view was fairly rapid but the store had to consider the reputational damage.

It is impossible to anticipate every crisis that can grip an organisation. Myer Grace Bros does have a plan now to deal with such a sensitive event but they also have strategies for prevention and damage limitation.

Every organisation faces the greatest harm from a serious incident aftermath. They may lack the financial and managerial resources needed to fully address a rapid recovery.

They have to consider a number of issues:

- Once a major incident has occurred, are there formal recovery plans in place to address employees, customers, the media, community groups and the government?
- Is there a sufficient relationship with police, fire and other emergency support organisations to assist the organisation with recovery?
- How will the organisation monitor post-traumatic stress in the aftermath across all its audiences?
- If a certain department has to be closed, how will the situation affect jobs or servicing the public?
- Have the legal issues related to investigations, coroner's inquests and inquiries been pre-planned?
- Are there emotional issues that have to be addressed related to neighbours, the local community and the wider public?

Preparing for these factors before things go wrong is far better than having to address them later. The environment for both the customer and the employee is different after a crisis.

## GOING FROM BOEING

In 1993, the Boeing Company faced a perceptional crisis in their role as the international leader in aerospace. Urgent recovery was foremost in their thinking when they faced the threat of a perceptual backlash as they eliminated something like 30 000 jobs.

Boeing obviously planned a careful recovery from this massive lay-off. Their recovery planning began some years before when they made sure that employees understood the direction of the company and were asked to contribute their ideas. A great deal of effort had been put into effective employee communication to gain greater co-operation. There was a policy in place to encourage knowledgeable and committed employees to act as ambassadors for the company.

So by the time Boeing had to cut jobs, there was already a well-heeled communication plan in place with employees. They were able to direct a program of openness and call on their already established reputation of concern for their employees. The spokesperson who led the communication thrust was the CEO, Frank Shrontz. In this crisis situation, once again this leadership role proved invaluable in giving employees and the majority of stakeholders the message.

The key to the recovery success was that employees were the first line of communication in a planned response. The CEO told it as it was and in doing so, waylaid a great deal of fear and apprehension. 'The reductions reflect the realities of the current market in the aerospace industry', he stated. 'We recognise the impact on our employees, their families and the communities we live and work in and we will try to minimise the effects.' (*Public Relations Journal*, December 1993.)

Boeing identified the threats well in advance, they understood the problems that would come with mass lay-offs and firings. And with each of these problems, they provided a broad range of recovery responses including a strategic program of individual employee notification. The approach to termination was through face-to-face meetings rather than soulless letters or memorandums. Boeing also offered a great deal of out-placement assistance, counselling services and provided a number of support services to make sure that staff had the utmost ability to search the job market effectively.

Here was a policy of honest communication based on the fact that the more Boeing's key audiences knew, the better the recovery for the whole corporation would be.

So the best crisis management planning needs to outline how management should address the needs of its people following a critical incident. Its people are those employees, customers and immediate stakeholders who are directly associated with the event.

## PEPSI'S RAPID RESPONSE RECOVERY

The major bottlers of soft drinks worldwide understand the need to link strategic recovery with crisis. Most have a central system to ensure that a crisis in one part of the world does not threaten another. Both internal and external impacts have to be identified well in advance and rapid recovery plans established and tested.

Never was a crisis management plan put more under the microscope in terms of recovery of both product and brand than Pepsi Cola's product tampering crisis in 1993. It all began on Thursday, 10 June 1993 when it was reported that an 82-year old man alleged he had discovered a syringe in a can of Diet Pepsi. This happened in early June and by 23 June, over 50 people from right across the United States had alleged they found a whole range of bits and pieces, including syringes, in similar cans of Pepsi.

Pepsi initially began to handle the crisis response locally according to their plan. Clear lines of communication with affected customers, government and the media were established and total transparency of the operation was offered. Tours of the factory, research background and quality control programs were offered around the clock.

But the rumour and innuendo had done its damage and copycat crazies were determined to turn this single unsubstantiated syringe story into an attack on big business.

The media was hot to trot with every investigative journalist in the United States leaping into action to be the first with the latest story. Pepsi was on the mat and the media were looking for blood. To recall or not to recall, that was the question.

The Pepsi crisis management team, headed by President Craig Weatherup, did have a plan to deal with the possibility of product recall and they certainly had a plan for recovery. But their product recall and recovery plan was very much about controlling the agenda and doing this with all the possible government support they could muster.

Obviously Pepsi believed they were in the right and that their manufacturing procedures in quality control could not be broken.

They could have been reactive to all the difficulties as they arose but they fought hard against that direction and concentrated on the key recovery issue. If the process of canning is safe, then we have to believe in ourselves and push that line.

So against the background of belief in the integrity of their system, they searched out strong government and intellectual support and they got it. The Food and Drug Administration (FDA), the Federal Bureau of Investigation (FBI), the police and the majority of government agencies clearly stood on the side of Pepsi's direction and showed a tough, attacking media that the public fears associated with this mass hysteria were absurd.

Pepsi took a hard, offensive line and the CEO spoke about the can as 'the most tamper-proof packaging in the food supply. We are 99.99% certain this didn't happen in Pepsi plants.'

And they showed it. They produced a video that showed the cannery in action and in close up detail, this video clearly indicated how product tampering of the type suggested was virtually impossible.

All of America was subjected to a massive program of video information on the Pepsi product review and tampering controls. The CEO led the public affairs program that accompanied the advertising and sat down with as many current affairs programs as possible to give reassurance from the top.

During this whole phantom crisis, faced with so many difficulties, Pepsi kept ahead of the demanding stakeholder agenda and stuck to its guns. They avoided the sensationalism of the media story. The falsehoods and irresponsibility of rumour that added so many copycat fakes to the event and they simply relied on a strong direction from an obviously tested team response.

The other factor that should be mentioned is the way in which Pepsi is said to have communicated internally throughout the crisis. They had well and truly identified that to continue or resume their business quickly, they had to have the confidence of their people. Their staff knew what was happening and it seems obvious that they were a crucial part of the recovery plan.

Pepsi lost US$40 million in sales during the product tampering scare, but this loss of market was soon recovered. It has to be said that they proved to themselves and their audiences that this scare could not be for real and recall was unrealistic. The Tylenol tampering for Johnson & Johnson was very real in its horror and therefore demanded an immediate recall. For the Australian biscuit company, Arnott's, again product tampering was possible and recall essential. In all these cases, the recovery relates very much to the threats that are identified in advance and a clear and decisive plan for prevention, control and damage limitation.

## INFRASTRUCTURE ENERGY CRISES

Deregulation and privatisation are fuelling the growth of infrastructure development around the world. While opportunities for investment and development are high in these areas, there is also the threat of a wide range of complex exposures. Australia and New Zealand have had their fair share of problems related to water and energy projects against the background of deregulation and privatisation.

In a series of infrastructure crises, the areas of efficient response and recovery became front page news and eventually led to major government investigations, inquiries and, in one case, a Royal Commission inquiry.

Rapid recovery from one serious infrastructure crisis was certainly on the mind of the state government in New South Wales, Australia during a major contamination scare in 1998. The giardia and cryptosporidium parasite had contaminated Sydney water with the fear of affecting three million people with severe diarrhoea and vomiting.

The Sydney Water Corporation temporarily closed down their water treatment plant, which had been isolated as the source of the contamination. The state government took control of the situation and managed the crisis. The Premier, Bob Carr, launched a major investigation and threatened to sack the managers who were responsible for the problem. This was all at a time when Sydney was preparing for the 2000 Olympic Games. Australia, of course, has a world reputation for its clean air and pristine wilderness.

As the rest of the world watched, Sydney Water's Chief Executive and a wide range of water experts struggled with the problem. Schools, hospitals and childcare centres went into damage control as children were highly vulnerable to the parasite. People were told to avoid consuming the water.

Sydney Water's CEO and Chairman both resigned and a legal nightmare for the government followed as organisations and businesses dealt with major disruption of production lines and huge bills for bottled water. Suggestions were made that Sydney Water was negligent in not preventing the contamination and that it had not advised consumers fast enough. Some media suggested that the water company had been slow to communicate and had waited two days before advising the public. Sydney major's newspaper, the *Sydney Morning Herald*, carried the headline: 'Safe water: The big lie'.

Two months later, following a major inquiry, the senior managers of the Sydney Water Corporation were severely criticised for their 'botched' handling of the crisis. The investigation found there were unacceptable delays in releasing effective warnings at the start of the crisis. They also found that there was inadequate testing after the parasite was identified and that there was a breakdown in decision-making at the executive level.

As part of the recovery process following the crisis, the Government announced a A\$15 rebate for Sydney Water users and a price freeze worth about A\$25 million. They cited the inconvenience caused by the giardia and cryptosporidium contamination.

But the population of Sydney and, as a result of the crisis a number of other Australian cities, are still recovering from the lack of confidence in what was once regarded as some of the cleanest drinking water in the world.

The complexity of the relationship between crisis management and recovery was never more obvious than in the Victorian gas crisis in September 1998, that in many ways developed into a potential national disaster in Australia. This crisis began as a plant explosion and a loss of gas supply to one of Australia's largest cities, Melbourne, and then moved to a situation that was highly critical of the condition of much of Australia's energy infrastructure.

It all began with a gas leak at the Esso (Exxon) Longford plant in country Victoria. Gas was leaking from the plant, and as maintenance workers were inspecting the problem, a gas explosion occurred triggering a fireball. The explosion killed 2 men and injured 8 others. Over 200 police, firefighters and emergency services specialists worked for many days to control the disastrous situation, assess damage and repair the crippled plant. This one plant provides the entire state's gas supply.

The gas crisis hit the car industry, plastics production, food and drink industries hard. Estimates were that the crisis would cost industry A\$35 million a day. Hospitals cancelled surgery and emergency plans were put in place to deliver essential services to the elderly and frail. Farmers had to dispense with millions of gallons of milk. Tens of thousands of workers were stood down as the shutdown affected the operations of many industries. Lawyers on behalf of businesses, unions and consumers, launched one of the biggest class actions in Australian legal history against Esso and other gas utilities.

In every crisis, there are opportunities. Thousands of people descended on major department stores in a buying frenzy. They searched out electric jugs, frying pans, heaters, burners, microwaves and barbecues. Solar showers were at a premium.

All businesses and households were ordered to turn off their gas at the meter and in a spectacular response, the public reacted quickly and stopped using hot water, central heating and cooking facilities. Communication from government and gas suppliers was excellent.

Then followed the process of plant recovery involving the isolation of the crippled plant and the testing of associated plants. During these efforts to restore the gas supply, the sombre and tragic funerals of the men killed posed a stark reminder of the severity of the incident.

When the plant was finally repaired and gas was slowly turned back on for business and industry initially, another potential crisis had to be faced by the supplier in the reconnection process. Amidst the fear that consumers may well cause an explosion in the reconnection process, consumers succeeded in restarting their supply with virtually no reports of injuries. A Royal Commission found Esso's failure to properly train its workers was the ultimate cause of Victoria's gas disaster.

## MGM HOTEL HORROR

Las Vegas is the centre of everything that is glamour and glitter and is the world gambling capital. This spectacularly action-packed and animated oasis in the Nevada Desert, home to so much fun, entertainment and wealth, became a nightmare of terror during one of the worst hotel fires in US history in 1980.

How does a hotel address the recovery issues when 84 people die and more than 600 hundred are injured in a US$50 million fire? It was a grand hotel with 2100 bedrooms and grand both in its profits and its entertainment.

On 21 November 1980, a kitchen incident, the cause of so many disasters, occurred in the basement of the building. Cooking fat set fire to the ceiling and a massive fireball blasted its way into the crowded casino. Gamblers died where they sat and others were caught as the entire casino was engulfed. But the worst was yet to come. Deadly noxious gases developed from the furniture and spread rapidly through the staircases to the rest of the building. Hundreds of guests were sleeping and completely unaware of the disaster below. There were no warnings, no smoke detectors and no alarm was heard.

People leapt to their death and others were rescued from the rooftop. Echoes of the 1974 Oscar-winning movie *The Towering Inferno* with its cold-blooded and grizzly exposé of people dying in a burning skyscraper.

The reality of this real event in Las Vegas was that a movie organisation owned the hotel and that organisation believed they had completed the hotel to the fire code standards of that time. Fire codes had been updated but fire drills were a fairly infrequent event. When fire drills were conducted most people took no notice of them (which unfortunately is true of many buildings today).

The disaster was given massive media coverage and MGM struggled with the problems of so many affected audiences—families of victims, the injured, the staff, the community of Las Vegas and the government. Shares in the MGM hotel corporation dropped as litigation began from the victims' families, amounting to almost US$2 billion.

The crisis escalated from an MGM hotel event to a Las Vegas state of mind. It was only three months later that gamblers had to flee another casino after a bomb scare and then there were three other hotel fires over the next six months, one at Caesar's Palace and two at the Hilton Hotel. The image of Las Vegas as the centre of fun, fashion and fortunes were replaced with fear, failings and fury. Revenues fell and perceptions plummeted.

While it could be suggested that strategic crisis management was not on the priority list of either MGM or Las Vegas in those days, it has to be said that both the hotel and the town made a remarkable recovery from the edge of destruction.

MGM led a dynamic recovery post-event. Decisions were made to deal with the avalanche of problems that came out of the event. Lawyers worked their way through masses of claims and punitive damages. MGM set out to stabilise the employees and community in the area and launched a massive rebuilding program which included a US$6 million computerised fire protection system.

They brought in experts from across the United States and each of the 2100 rooms was finished with heat-activated sprinklers, smoke detectors, ceiling alarm and speaker systems controlled around the clock. The hotel was riddled with safety devices and government agencies were linked in a whole new set of guidelines. In true Hollywood style, film stars from the MGM stable were brought in to convince everyone that Las Vegas and MGM hotels were safe places to be. Gene Kelly, the veteran Hollywood star, hosted a film within the hotel for all guests on what to do in a fire situation.

This was a case of recovery after the event with very little pre-planning for such a disaster. In those days, this was more often the case. There have been big changes both in company policy and public regulations since then. Litigation is a much bigger issue and overall, society is a lot more unforgiving and demanding. Recovery must be part of pre-planning or organisations will simply not be able to respond rapidly to shifting public values and rising demands for accountability.

## THE RECOVERY RESPONSE

Actions have to occur in the immediate hours following an incident —this is the recovery time that matters. It is very often forgotten that recovery involves dealing with the non-physical injuries. Stress-related disabilities now account for 14% of workers' compensation claims and are twice as costly as the average physical injury claim.

Those who witness the event and those who try to rescue injured employees very often suffer emotional injuries, which are covered by workers' compensation. It is a known fact that stress-related disabilities, particularly those caused by a traumatic event at the work-place, can disrupt work performance and devastate good employees for years.

In the same manner, if the threat identified is the serious injury or death of an employee, the recovery goals will include minimising the impact on other employees and next of kin, in an understanding and compassionate manner, and rehabilitating the injured employee back to the workforce.

Likewise, the recovery strategy for serious injury, for example, will cover such things as an employment rehabilitation plan (including counselling and physical rehabilitation); ongoing contact and support; arranging insurance payments in a timely fashion; assessing other avenues of appropriate financial assistance; and creating a timetable for return to work.

The recovery strategy for a workplace death will include a range of actions that must be handled sensitively and well. These will cover maintaining contact with next of kin; assistance with moving the body to the place of burial and with funeral arrangements, if requested by next of kin; counselling for next of kin and affected employees; financial assistance; and help with statutory enquiries, among others.

# ENVIRONMENTAL RESPONSES

Where the potential threat is serious damage to the natural environment, the objective must be to contain the damage to a defined area, and to work with regulatory authorities and community and special interest groups to determine the recovery strategies. Issues to be considered include legal and regulatory compliance, insurance coverage, rehabilitation of the environment, community input and media management.

# RELOCATION PLAN

A particular aspect of crisis management planning that is often overlooked is the fact that crises can prevent you from operating out of your normal premises as a result of a natural disaster, a man-made disaster, a systems collapse or an energy failure. All of a sudden there is a need to move to temporary or new premises.

During a crisis exercise workshop, one of the first questions often put to the crisis management team is: where would you manage the crisis from if you could not manage it from here?

Probably the most important element of any team leader's responsibility is to ensure that the company can continue to function even though it experiences a major incident or accident.

Losing your building, office, site, location or precinct, should be an essential element of planning. The fundamental element in this situation is the back-up premises. The time to prepare for this is well before an emergency occurs, not if an emergency occurs.

As mentioned, in one of the worst terrorist attacks in the City of London, the Commercial Union building was literally blown to pieces. This head office building was rendered totally inoperable. Almost immediately, the huge British insurance company was able to locate alternate premises.

Their temporary crisis management team moved to a specifically identified location and managed the crisis issues from that office, while the company set up an empty building to move all their staff and management into over a weekend. Telephones, computers, facsimiles and communication systems were rapidly brought on-line and staff were contacted about the move to this new location and briefed on the changing situation that had rendered their normal office unusable. Their recovery plan allowed the firm to get back in business virtually over a weekend.

Some organisations have made their crisis management team and its facilities portable. In other words, they have prepared a comprehensive crisis and recovery transportable unit for dealing with a situation that prevents them from using their normal crisis control room. The portable unit allows them to respond quickly at any location with the appropriate equipment and supplies such as mobile telephones, manuals, contact lists, two-way radios, maps and checklists.

Organisations that want to keep their losses to a minimum and need to take immediate control of a crisis situation, should identify alternative premises well in advance. These premises can take a number of forms:

1. Close sites. These can be alternative and temporary premises close by. Usually these premises are linked with sufficient, immediate communication access to the organisation's main line of information. This allows a switch-over to support the database and telephone system.

2. Friendly neighbours. This is a back-up site for full or temporary operation. It might not have the immediate technical communication lines to link computers and telephones, but can give immediate access to key stakeholders and is still within close access to the original operation.

3. Corporate regional office location. This can be one of your organisation's offices that is located some distance from the original organisation location. It provides 'hot', instantaneous links to databases, telephones, facsimiles and e-mail, but takes you away from the location of your crisis.

4. The portable location. This is more a mobile situation which has been pre-organised to give you an ongoing temporary back-up facility. It can be set up from suitcases or a van or bus and can provide the necessary switch-over to back up databases, telephones and communication systems. This unit is often used by the transport industry and emergency services for managing protracted events that happen at distant and inaccessible locations.

# CONTROL POINTS

☐ The minute a crisis is declared, the recovery phase runs parallel.

☐ Once a threat has been realised, it can be mitigated against by recovery planning.

☐ The recovery plan should be regularly tested and reviewed to retain its robustness.

☐ Recovery needs to consider plans for employees, customers, media, community groups and government.

☐ Recovery plans may involve long-lasting legal issues, investigations and inquests.

☐ Infrastructure crises and emergencies can involve secondary crises in their recovery.

☐ Recovery must be part of crisis planning so organisations can respond rapidly to shifting public values and rising demands for accountability.

☐ Recovery strategies for workplace injuries and deaths involve counselling, financial assistance and ongoing rehabilitation.

☐ Environmental recovery in crisis must be designed to contain damage and to identify regulatory authorities and community groups for ongoing consultation.

☐ Consideration needs to be given for relocation of office or plant in recovery planning.

# 9

# CREATING YOUR PLAN

The storm was unusually aggressive. While the Captain knew that flying at this height was, at this stage of the journey, the most comfortable for the passengers, there was excessive turbulence, which this aircraft should and would handle well. That was the benefit of the A300–B4 Airbus. She had been put to the test throughout the world in the toughest weather conditions. Suddenly she shuddered as an air pocket caused the two General Electric jet engines to whine and she suddenly dropped from 9500 metres to 7000 metres. The Captain and First Officer were struggling with the controls as the myriad of lights on the control board flashed and warning sirens sounded throughout the cabin. The Captain checked his manual and followed clear instructions to stabilise the dive. The aircraft stabilised and the 200 passengers eased back in their seats. The Captain was in control again.

Knowing what to do when things go wrong is a strategic challenge for any individual or organisation. Having a plan to follow makes the difference—developing easy to follow guidelines helps in the mobilisation of crisis teams and having checklists for them to follow gets the team on top of the response.

Not a week goes by where a newspaper in virtually every city in every country has news of a crisis of some kind. From issues of public health to major accidents, energy collapses, natural disasters, environmental spills and the ever-increasing urban terrorist or criminal acts.

These call for rapid response and I have specified throughout this book the need to have conditions favourable to handling a crisis in place before it happens. Invariably, most organisations have effective emergency planning but they overlook the importance of developing and testing a crisis plan in its entirety. What is the ideal plan? How much can be done in advance in terms of planning? What is the best way to develop and keep your plan current and effective?

If you have ever been through a personal crisis of any kind, you will understand how important a set of guidelines and directions are. If you have ever rushed to find a spare set of car keys to urgently drive someone to hospital or searched for a street directory or telephone directory to find a doctor. If you have fumbled for an emergency service number in the middle of the night or tried to give instructions to someone on how to escape from the upstairs of a burning home, then you have had a taste of the need to be prepared.

It is no different from the confusion that often occurs in a major business or government organisation. Once a crisis hits, people want and need direction. They either respond with the knowledge of what to do, or they head off in all different directions having a wide range of views of how the situation should be handled.

It can take hours and days to control the confusion. Valuable minutes can be lost, while managers attempt to give a broad range of instructions to a wide range of people who are still coming to terms with the pressure and the threats. But once a team of dedicated thinkers and doers has a crisis plan to work to, then and only then do we develop a decision-making process that can deal with a difficult situation. The barrage of urgent events are looked at logically and related to experience and processes. The group or team is driven by a planned process. The problems are pinpointed and the crisis response is based on experienced decisions which protect the organisation.

This chapter focuses on providing a useful plan and checklist offering strategies for prevention, control and effective response. The critical requirement in crisis management planning is that everyone involved in the response has the same terms of reference. There has to be a central logic to the process. The CEO, the receptionist and the plant operator, should be able to work around the same holistic approach in any location at any time of the day or night.

Unless the organisation has a written, well-defined, systematic plan with clear roles and responsibilities defined, then frankly, come the next crisis, your response will be slow and ineffective.

# ESSENTIALS IN THE PLANNING PROCESS

In determining how to go about the development of a crisis management and recovery plan, it is important to consider that the plan must have the approval of the people at the top; it should be versatile, flexible and easy to understand; it needs to be adaptable across every location in the organisation; contain a review and maintenance process; provide checklist responses for most of the key threats at that office, site or location; specify roles and responsibilities; and include a methodology for continual improvement through planned testing and review.

1. The planning process must be endorsed by the CEO and the board. If crisis management is to be taken seriously and installed efficiently, it must come from and be part of the people who run the business. After all, in the end, it is those people who will have to manage the crisis when it reaches its most ferocious point.

2. The crisis plan has to be part of company policy and those who are involved in its creation, instalment and ongoing delivery, need to have their accountability listed in their job description.

3. The plan must be simple and easy to use. At a time of crisis people have less time and less attention span and don't want to be confused by longwinded, wordy, jargon-filled instructions. The plan needs common language that simply and easily identifies the goals and objectives, the methods of delivery and implementation, and the ongoing evaluation and continuity. Short- and long-term goals are essential if it is to survive and flourish.

4. Accountability is essential. Senior management personnel must be given the time and the authority to be accountable for the delivery of this plan. Once a manager is given the role of organising a crisis management plan, this person should be supported and assisted in their review by a dedicated, professional, outside crisis management consultancy. This outside consultancy will assist in a reliable, audit process with measurable reviews linked to the company's audit procedures.

5. A crisis management budget needs to be set and approved. Any crisis management plan that is going to last needs a budget. Instituting and delivering the plan will have a cost. Some organisations may prefer to link the crisis management budget with the risk management function. Others may associate it with good corporate governance and build it into the corporate and public

policy area. Some may prefer it to be associated with the public affairs or human resources function. Manufacturing companies may link their crisis management plan with their marketing and product recall function. Regardless of its divisional line of responsibility, a budget needs to be developed and reviewed annually.

6. The crisis management plan must be capable of application at every office, branch, site and location. Just as head office has a role to play in managing corporate and business crises, so do those offices, branches, sites and locations in managing the same responsibility on-the-spot. When a crisis happens, it must be handled quickly where it happens. If the location or site is not given the authority to act, valuable time will be lost and ultimately the control and the agenda may move to another negative party.

7. Employees must be involved in the crisis management process. As mentioned earlier, if you do not involve your employees in the crisis management loop, you lose valuable allies. When the crisis hits, you may need additional support in many areas. Giving employees a basic understanding of the plan, means they are ready to help prepare for a crisis and help respond when it happens.

8. Insist on contractors sharing your crisis management methodology. When hit by a crisis, the contractor should immediately become part of the crisis response under your plan. To have a major contractor working to a different plan or system can cause a mixed response or, at worst, an alternative response. The media, regulators and lawyers will use the lack of continuity in responses against you.

9. Make sure your crisis management plan has clear links or triggers from your emergency, safety, health and environmental issues and product recall plans. There should be precise trigger points where any of those elements turns to the crisis phase.

10. Establish an effective link with a communications company capable of providing you with an efficient call-out process, i.e. a 24-hour paging system so that your crisis management team can be reached anywhere, anytime. Make sure that this call-out system has an early warning system to other parts of your organisation should the crisis escalate to them.

11. Make sure the plan clearly indicates formatted recording systems so that precise records are kept of any incident. Back this up with sufficient information technology to ensure its security.

12. Every plan needs to have a maintenance process. It must be acceptable to internal auditors, outside auditors, senior management and recognised by the board of directors.

13. Education of team members and support groups needs to be an ongoing process. Once the CORE team members have been educated about their roles and responsibilities and the support team has identified their part in the response, it is necessary to test and review these people regularly. Most teams are tested two or three times a year with either desk-top exercises or full-scale simulations.

14. Every crisis team at every location will rely enormously on resources. Control room facilities such as whiteboards, facsimiles, telephones and two-way radios, are all part of the resource kit. Items such as transport need to be considered too. Dedicated aircraft may be required to rush a crisis team to a specific location. Security support and psychological counselling are often needed.

15. How do you set a budget? Crisis planners need to think in terms of modules. There are five phases in the costing process:

    (a) The audit. Whether this is done internally or with outside assistance, it is critical to review the whole of the organisation's crisis preparedness. The cost of this element depends entirely on how many locations and how deep the review. What is really critical is that the areas of exposure are identified and the present response capability is reviewed in light of the company's current risk management or emergency plan.

    (b) Developing the plan and the team. This development phase needs to be facilitated through a number of workshops (depending on the size of the organisation and the extent of the exposure). These workshops should deliver the roles and responsibilities of the team and a precise response plan for the key threats across the organisation. It needs to be seamless and simple. The cost of outside specialists and their travel to all company locations is a key factor. Crisis budget planners also need to consider the amount of time this activity will take in relation to management involvement.

    (c) The actual plan and manual. This can get right out of control if it is handled by amateurs. Plan development costs will escalate unless there is a precise project timeline developed for writing the plan and distributing it throughout the business. If you are doing it internally, then budgets need to be related very much to the time it will take people to detail the plan in relation to corporate controls. Simple, easy to understand plans in the long-term are the most cost effective because they are easier to communicate and easier to test. Consideration should be given to developing internal software systems for

**153**

the plan and manual, so that reviewing and testing processes can be made inexpensively through either Intranet or e-mail.

(d) Annual testing procedure that is used to review the system. This again can be made cost effective if the various tests are simplified and become part of the company or organisational audit. Desk-top exercises, whether they be presented on software or facilitated 'live', need to be costed as regular events. The larger simulations or full-scale exercises are an essential part of the crisis management process and can cost anywhere from US$10 000 to $100 000, depending entirely on the size of the site or business being reviewed and the amount of interplay between emergency services, participants and facilities. While the planning can take weeks or months and the results and reports can be extensive, at the same time they provide vital assistance in improving organisational readiness.

(e) The final phase is the cost of ongoing maintenance of the plan and the linking of the plan with other organisational skills and regulatory requirements. Someone has to take the role of implementation and make sure that the crisis plan supports the business plan. Someone has to continue to advise on the crisis plan development and improvement. Someone has to report on plan progress to the CEO, board, risk manager, legal advisors and so on. This internal manager needs to be costed into the process. There may be a further cost of an outside specialist to assist in the initial development and facilitation of the crisis plan.

An independent crisis management consultant can often supply unique processes and solutions that have been tried and tested by other organisations and proved in the field. Outside specialists can also often assist in the more accurate budgeting of the crisis management and recovery installation process.

## THE *HERALD OF FREE ENTERPRISE* FERRY DISASTER

There is never a greater need for a plan than during a transport crisis. These critical incidents often happen at a difficult and distant location, can involve many victims and rely enormously on urgent and rapid information flow.

On Friday, 6 March 1987, in the early evening, almost 200

people died as the *Herald of Free Enterprise* ferry capsized near the Zeebrugge Harbour in Belgium. The Zeebrugge emergency plan had only been in place for a few months before the accident and there had been no overall testing of the plan, but there were actions lists in place. Importantly, like so many crises, there is that total disbelief that this kind of event could ever happen in the first place.

From many accounts, the emergency was handled particularly well and the response and rescue could be described as a considerable success. Essential plans were followed efficiently and a rapid response was achieved.

The watchman of a barge in the harbour watched as the lights of the ferry virtually turned upside down. He gave the emergency call and then the barge headed off to assist. Lifeboats and tugs were launched to assist. Passengers were struggling from the ferry, which was lying half emerged on a sandbank.

There was a massive response from emergency headquarters in Brugge and an enormous search commenced and rescue helicopters were mobilised, as were a number of ships sailing in the nearby channel. Medical and ambulance support were put on standby immediately and additional Red Cross support was linked to the response.

The company's early media response was that the ferry had hit the harbour wall as it departed. This harbour wall accident became the headline in newspaper and television reports for days.

But the company who owned the ferry was not enthusiastic about giving any more details, so the investigative media dug deeper and found that in fact the ferry had not closed its bow doors on its departure from the port. The reason for the ferry's demise was that a massive amount of water had capsized the ship. There was a media outcry about the company, Townsend Thorensen, and its cover-up and claims of people dying because of the company's greed. The image of the ferry company collapsed.

The case in point was that there may have been a sufficient plan to deal with the emergency, but there was no plan in place to handle the crisis situation. Rescue teams may have saved more than 350 passengers and crew during the first hours after the capsizing of the ferry, but nothing could save the confrontation of the media and the owners of the ferry when repeated requests for information were denied. Nothing could save the future of that ferry line when it became clear that vital information had been withheld.

John P. Heck from the Ministry of the Interior, The Civil

Emergency Planning, The Hague, in his review of the Zeebrugge ferry disaster makes an important point of the plausibility of this crisis and need for risk assessment:

"A particular point I would like to stress—and which appears directly relevant for the pre-*Herald of Free Enterprise* disaster risk assessments on the chances of a ferry capsizing in front of the port of Zeebrugge—is that crises are not events that present themselves like a bolt from the blue. Under normal circumstances, most crises seem highly unlikely to happen. But the risk of a crisis can never be ruled out completely, either because the chance that a specific type of disaster will strike one day is far from negligible, or because the consequences of a crisis, even if it is unlikely that this will ever take place, are unacceptable.

"Therefore, public authorities should not only not pursue an ostrich policy. They must also make realistic risk analyses. Subsequently, they can, of course, always hope for the best but, at the same time, they ought to plan for the worse". (Rosenthal, U. and Pijnenburg, B., *Crisis Management and Decision Making* (1991)).

## CRISES AT SPORTING VENUES

Most sporting venues have an emergency plan for fire and evacuation as do most entertainment complexes. Thousands of people gathered in arenas, stadiums or theatres can be a crisis waiting to happen. The evacuation management of these people can turn the reputation of a sport or theatrical production into a horrific, memorable event that affects gate sales for many years to come.

The British tragedy at Hillsborough in 1989 was a shocking event involving thousands of people in a mass of confusion and terror that was being televised live. Five thousand Liverpool football fans watching a semi-final at the Hillsborough stadium were, because of over-crowding, put into a position of being unable to get through turnstiles. The crowds were redirected into a tunnel which forced them to an area that was virtually caged off. Emergency gates were not open and crowds were pushed up against wire caging. Many people were killed and injured and the media turned the tragedy into an even greater disaster by printing dreadful pictures of victims' suffering in the crush. Rumour and innuendo related to the drunken state of the fans and the difficulty the police had to face in dealing with them. In fact, the crowd was a victim of lack of planning and bureaucratic bungling.

The South Yorkshire Police did have a plan for re-routing the crowds, but the plan, rather than protecting people, was very much aimed at protecting the football ground from being invaded by people. There was not a plan it seems for a major crisis of panic and chaos.

In another sporting incident in 1998, a peaceful, annual international sailing classic, turned into one of the world's most serious rescue operations in yachting history. The Sydney to Hobart Yacht Race is held annually after Christmas. The yachts sailed out of picturesque Sydney Harbour on a sunny, beautiful day, but as they made their way along the East Coast of Australia, a shocking storm hit the 115 boats. Winds of 80 knots whipped up huge waves. The yacht race became a race for survival as a huge rescue operation was mounted by the Australian Maritime Safety Authority.

Certainly plans were in place to assist in the rescue should some of the boats get into trouble, but no in-depth plans were in place to deal with mass havoc caused by wild seas, snapping masts and the tossing of many of the crews into the sea. Thirty fixed-wing aircraft and five Navy and Air Force aircraft, together with police and rescue helicopters, were joined by Australian Navy warships. Six people were killed and many were injured.

The world watched the CNN and BBC television coverage as the massive rescue took place. In one particular piece of television coverage, a live camera on one of the yachts showed the intensity of the waves smashing on to the deck as the mast was snapped and one of the yacht's crew members was swept over the side.

The emergency plan for this 1998 race was without doubt responsible for saving many lives. However, the investigation that followed asked the question of whether the race should have been abandoned earlier when it was known that the weather was going to develop to a critical situation.

Questions about the experience of the crews and the capability of individual crew members for dealing with the intensity of severe weather conditions are still being reviewed by coronial and yachting officials. Lawyers acting for the families of deceased and injured sailors were talking of suing the race organisers for not calling a halt to the race earlier.

Certainly this famous yacht race will survive the crisis, but the search for answers into this most devastating yacht race will demand a new planning process to deal with the safety of future yacht races facing the threat of severe weather.

# PLAN CONTENT

The crisis management plan is a document that lays out the framework and system for the preparation of, and response and recovery to, a major event. The plan should provide a comprehensive and integrated structure that can operate across an organisation seamlessly. It should be simple and easy to apply to an organisation in terms of implementation, education, maintenance and continuous improvement. Importantly, it should contain a common terminology so that any manager, at any location and at any time, can understand directions of what to do and how to do it.

Essentially, this must not be written as an emergency plan. It is not designed to arrest a fire, or deal with first-aid, or a gas or chemical leak. It is more about safeguarding people, assets, market share, cash flow and loss of brand or corporate image. This plan is about business continuity and control of corporate issues. And it is about corporate recovery. It should provide a seamless process across the organisation.

The plan should have three sections. The first section will outline what the crisis team does immediately. The second section will detail all the necessary processes through to resolution, and will include individual team member actions, the recently identified list of key threats and a checklist of recommended responses. The final section will contain a contact directory, and all pro formas of letters, media releases, advertisements, call registers, and a log of events.

In addition to the plan, a set of action checklists will provide the team with essential items that have to be dealt with in a crisis situation.

## Style

The plan should be produced in an easy to use, fast response format, employing convenient page numbering and cross-referencing.

## Content

The plan would have the following structure and contents.

- Immediate action guide—What to do first:
    - Notification to crisis management team
    - Crisis management team mobilisation
    - Interaction with emergency control centre
    - Initial response guidelines
- Document control:
    - Issues and amendment procedures
    - Revision and distribution
- Introduction:
    - Crisis policy, purpose and scope
    - Format of plan
- Organisation, roles and responsibilities:
    - Crisis management teams
    - Support logistics
    - Response checklists
- Crisis response:
    - Serious accident or injury
    - Product contamination/extortion
    - Major product recall
    - Major industrial dispute
    - Armed intrusion
    - Hostage and siege
- Communications:
    - Internal
    - External
- Facilities:
    - Crisis control room and alternatives
- Crisis control procedures:
    - Log of events
    - Reception and switchboard
    - Media call log information
    - Communicating with employees
    - Computer security
    - Recovery plan
- Contact directory:
    - CM&R teams
    - Management support
    - Chairman and board
    - Government
    - Emergency services
    - Media

- Appendices:
    Log of events form
    Crisis telephone call register
    Media call log form
    Reference material, maps, plans, etc.
    Media aids—fast facts, pro forma press releases.

The essentials of a basic plan are as follows.

- *Organisation.* This should outline how the plan will work across your particular business or operation. It should include management philosophy towards crisis management and its link with emergency planning, issues management, product recall and security planning. It should outline who, in the corporate organisation, is responsible for the whole crisis management plan and emphasise the legal and regulatory requirements of the plan. It needs sufficient planning information about human resources support, reporting to senior management and essential items such as document control and security and confidentiality of material. Details as to who the plan is distributed to and the necessary plan revision instructions should be defined. A crisis management manual needs to be defined under this organisational heading. Details of the contents and its distribution and validation should be confirmed.
- *Team management.* This lists how the team is structured and who should be in it. It needs to identify the different task forces necessary to deal with responses at every level. It needs to identify the structure of teams, the qualification of those people involved and their roles and responsibilities.

    The plan should clearly outline how teams interrelate during a crisis, lines of authority and core responsibilities. The leadership issue needs to be laid down and clear authority has to be detailed. Back-up and support teams and systems should be described. These procedures also need to detail who is responsible for the alarm or call-out (the required actions and authorities to mobilise the team). (See Chapter 3–Creating and Managing a Crisis Team.)
- *Crisis 'threats' identification.* This element details the framework for threat assessment in order to provide a suitable response. It recognises the vulnerabilities of the organisation—the types of crises that could occur to a company or organisation. It should provide a clear definition about worst case scenarios. It needs to provide a process of identifying a wide range of threat exposures that may impact on the organisation. It should also outline the

importance of these threat analyses to local conditions. Head office should have its own set of threats and then each site and location should identify its own dedicated set of threats. This process should be documented as an annual requirement. These procedures should provide a description of the level and classification of the event in a common standard across the organisation.

- *Crisis response procedures.* This step identifies how responses to the above threats are detailed. It confirms the necessary actions of the team relative to the response and control of the crisis. It sets out how the checklist of responses is listed. It determines how to go about identifying the most efficient response strategies. It should provide guidelines for the action responses of teams and support groups.
- *Command centre and communication facilities support.* The purpose of these procedures is to locate and equip a central command centre for each crisis team. This item should identify a standard plan for the location and type of control room for the management of an incident.

    These procedures should detail a secure location and lay out the necessary equipment to assist crisis teams in being kept informed and providing information regarding crisis events.

    They should provide the equipment to interface with incidents in the field and the technical equipment details to communicate outside the location during crisis incidents. It should also provide facilities for logging and minuting the course of events.

    Communication hardware and software should be detailed, particularly related to portable equipment and temporary back-up systems. It should detail external emergency, medical and security support availability.
- *Information procedures.* The requirement of this component of the plan is to list the methods and techniques to provide information about what has happened to a wide range of stakeholders. It should list the methodology of the message agenda control. It should identify internal and external audiences, including employees, the media, the community, government and so on. It should confirm the process of corporate transparency related to information flow and detail.

    It should identify the spokesperson's role and guidelines for dealing with the media, victims' families, distressed personnel, investigators and security incidents.
- *Training and retraining standards.* The training requirements need to be qualified in terms of teaching and education, evaluation of

needs, plan instruction, group workshops, desk-top exercises and full-scale simulations. This procedure should identify training policies, definitions of instructors' competency and an overview of auditing procedures for the training plan.

# THE MANUAL

The manual is the essential reference document. It has to include the most current up-to-date information about what to do and who to contact. It has to be available. During a recent crisis event investigation at a major industrial site, the post-evaluation team was reviewing all the administrative considerations relating to the crisis. The idea was to provide an overview of the lessons learnt in the implementation of the crisis plan.

The point of reference was how fast was the response and how efficient were the communications during the critical early hours of the event.

The team was a new team and had only been partly trained in crisis management, although the process was well-established within the organisation. The team leader was also the registered site manager and had yet to be instructed in the crisis management response process.

'How did you cope initially?' the investigator asked. 'Well, we seemed to get things going fairly quickly. Once we knew what to do, we did it.' He looked a little shy and said: 'The trouble was, we couldn't find the crisis manual ... I mean we knew it was somewhere but we couldn't remember where.' The investigator continued: 'How long did it take you to find it?' Came the rapid reply: 'Oh, up to 15 minutes.'

Finding the manual, reading the manual and understanding the manual in a crisis is no easy task. It is then, and only then, that you know that the manual must provide the fastest possible response checklist. It has to show you in simple, easy words what has to be done and it has to give you a framework for action. Critical to the ability of any team leader is the ability to comprehend the manual. The ideal manual should be thin (easy to lift) but fat in fast information.

The checklists and contact lists need to be printed in good, readable type. Even the most poor-sighted person should be able to read the instructions without glasses in the poorest of light.

# MAINTAINING THE PLAN—
# CONTINUAL IMPROVEMENT

Nothing stays the same. Business changes rapidly and so too do the threats that surround operations. Because crisis management and recovery planning depends very much on the currency of information, plans must be subject to continual maintenance and review. It is necessary to regularly review the threat analysis, implement changes to contact lists and update procedures to ensure viability.

Plans have a habit of growing old and gathering dust until one day they are needed and then they prove hopelessly out-of-date. In one case of a serious chemical leak, the crisis management team called for assistance from their crisis management plan and found that the contact numbers of the team were all seriously out-of-date. Many of the team had changed and therefore their after-hours telephone numbers were not listed. When the team leader attempted to call the central operations control room, the retort came on the other end of the telephone as: 'Hello, canteen'. When they moved into the response mode after considerable trouble finding the team, they discovered that there was no reference as to what to do related to this chemical problem. In the last 18 months, new chemicals had been introduced to the site and the crisis management team had not evaluated these new threats and added them to the response structure.

Other problems were related to security issues. When the outside emergency services support arrived, they were held up at the entrance to the plant by newly appointed security officers whose instructions were not to grant entrance to any special vehicle without prior agreement by the plant manager. Security plans had not been integrated into crisis and emergency management plans and therefore response to dealing with a serious hazard was slowed up considerably.

So in order to maintain a superior information flow and achieve optimum responses in a crisis situation, plans and procedures have to be updated regularly and cross-referenced.

## Responsibility

It has been stated earlier in this book that it is the responsibility of the team leader to ensure the efficient development of a plan. They need to ensure that the administrative considerations related to the regular update of the basic plan and supporting material actually happens. One person needs to be given clear responsibility for the review and regular updating of relevant information.

## Distribution of the plan

Who receives copies of the plan? How many copies? The person chosen to control the ongoing maintenance of the plan needs to also be responsible for the control and distribution. It is important that copies of the plan be coded and kept secure because the information enclosed in most cases is of a sensitive and confidential nature. A method of document control should be established and the methodology should be subject to annual corporate review and audit.

## Language

The way in which plans are written, and the language of the procedures needs to be defined accurately. Because emergency planning standards and regulations change from region to state to country, it is essential that a common language is used across each location plan. The way in which names, titles, telephone numbers and emergency terminology are expressed should all be of a common standard.

It is also essential that the language integrates across other plans used by the organisation. It is no use in the early stages of a crisis for emergency teams and crisis teams to be arguing over the language of plan implementing procedures.

The following should never happen:

First voice: 'Hello. This is a serious situation. I am declaring a Level Three situation.'

Second voice: 'You mean Level Four.'

First voice: 'I said Level Three. We have a fire with injured personnel and a chemical spill.'

Second voice: 'That is surely a Level Four by my book.'

First voice: 'There is no such thing as a Level Four.'

Second voice: 'They're not Levels, anyway. They are categorised as Stages.'

First voice: 'Who put this plan together anyway?'

## Outside consultants

Preparing and organising a detailed crisis management and recovery plan and manual is a big job. While your organisation may be able to workshop and plan strategies for prevention and response in dealing with crisis and work through the prevention and recovery phases, the actual documentation of the plan needs to be accurate and efficient. Getting the standards right and establishing a common terminology all based around quality legal and regulatory considerations, requires a dedicated project manager.

Most organisations have neither the time nor the experience to complete the plan and the written manuals and they, therefore, choose to engage outside consultants to prepare and organise the work.

When choosing a consultant to put together your crisis management and recovery plan, it is important they have the relevant experience in preparing similar plans for chemical, pharmaceutical, manufacturing, transportation or whatever field relates to your specific area of operation. It is important that they share their experience of implementing complete crisis management plans, not just those related to the specific area of public relations or security or environmental planning.

Crisis management plans need to be designed and set up by crisis management consultants who can offer the full skills base that covers response to accidents, product problems, business issues, ethical issues and security. The application of the plan must not be restricted in its coverage.

## POST-INCIDENT REVIEW— LEARNING FROM CRISES

No simulation or crisis management exercise can ever replace the real thing. When a real crisis occurs, most aspects of the crisis management plan will be applied, but there will be many more critical issues and intricacies that will appear.

It goes without saying that the goal of this book is to provide strategies to protect the company's operations and reputation by providing a safety net. But the identification of possible holes in the safety net can be best discovered after a review of a real crisis situation.

In Chapter 11, we provide a recipe for setting up a crisis exercise. How to create an interactive simulation and give the crisis teams and their decision-makers an understanding of the stages of crisis and skills in response techniques.

The simulation or exercise concludes with an evaluation and critique where responses are examined and roles and responsibilities reviewed. The aim of these crisis exercises is to improve the effectiveness of the teams in managing a crisis, at the same time as reviewing the crisis manual and the various human and technical resources that assist the process.

A real event, aside from its serious consequences, can offer greater lessons, particularly related to the complex issues of communication, interactiveness and stress.

Any post-crisis evaluation must be done relatively quickly after the event. The real value of what has happened, and how crisis teams responded, can be only be learnt while memories are alert to the central issues of the response. The purpose of the post-crisis evaluation is not to investigate the cause of the incident nor items such as emergency response, product recall action or security performance, but more how the crisis management team performed in its role. Was the crisis identified effectively? Was the team called out efficiently? Could the team respond immediately and was the response effective?

Post-crisis evaluation is about managing and controlling the corporate issues related to the future of the business. Therefore, it is not interested in the front-line issues of fire fighting or clean-ups. The following 15 items need to be addressed:

1. A narrative of the actual event. What happened, why and how and what caused the event?
2. How was the response managed by the crisis management team? How did the response relate to operational procedures? What was the decision-making process based on?
3. Were resources adequate? Where did they fail and how could they have been improved?
4. Is the organisation still under threat from the problem or similar problems?
5. What were the unintended consequences that came out of the original incident?
6. Were there any barriers to communication?
7. Were all stakeholders advised effectively? If not, what were the problems?
8. Was there sufficient co-operation with outside agencies (emergency services, government, etc.)?
9. Were the plan, manual and procedures useful? Where could they be improved?
10. Were human resource issues and employee communication handled efficiently?
11. Were there any barriers to crisis response from senior management?
12. Were legal issues dealt with efficiently?

13. Was the spokesperson's role effective? Were messages continual and consistent?
14. How was business continuity and recovery managed? What were the problems?
15. What has been put in place in the short-term and the long-term to prevent this crisis from happening again?

This post-evaluation needs to be carried out by either outside consultants or a senior management team and preferably not by the crisis management team. It is designed to improve operations, decision-making, plans, skills and to ensure the crisis management team has done its job.

The post-evaluation team needs to interview the crisis management team, management executives, employees, consultants and external personnel involved in the crisis.

A post-evaluation project is no easy task. While it has to be done as soon as possible after the crisis has occurred, it needs time to be reviewed and put into context. The project team needs the support of the chief executive and senior management and commitment has to be given to ensure that the lessons learnt can eventually be incorporated in the overall crisis managing planning process.

## CONTROL POINTS

☐ Having a plan to follow makes the difference. Developing easy-to-follow guidelines helps in mobilisation and response.

☐ Once a crisis hits, people want and need direction.

☐ Unless the organisation has a written, well-defined systematic plan with clear roles and responsibilities, response will be slow.

☐ The planning process must be endorsed by the CEO.

☐ All plans must be simple and easy to use.

☐ Insist on contractors sharing the crisis management planning methodology.

☐ Plans need a regular maintenance process to keep them current.

☐ In addition to the plan, a set of action checklists will provide the team with essential responses.

☐ Plans need to set out training and retraining programs to keep teams in touch with procedures.

☐ The manual and checklists must be easy to locate.

☐ Lessons learnt from real crises and crisis exercises should be incorporated in the plan following post-evaluation.

# 10

## PRODUCT PROBLEMS, LITIGATION AND RECALL

The product launch attracted huge media coverage. They called it the toy of the year. This plump, cuddly teddy bear was every child's dream and every parent's perfect gift. It was Christmas and the retail stores were selling 'Tom Teddy' by the thousands. The company (one of the world's largest toy manufacturers) had a new product hit and with the right research and development and efficient pricing and branding, the retailers picked it up quickly. Advertising campaigns had swamped the country for two months. A week before Christmas, a doctor from one of the city's children's hospitals called the Product Manager: 'The dye in "Tom Teddy's" fur could well be toxic.' One child was seriously ill and calls were now coming in from across the country. They put the recall on hold and waited. The TV current affairs programs began their attack as more children were admitted to hospital. The company's long history of successes was now put at stake as women's magazines across the country accused them of irresponsibility. Now the government insisted on an urgent recall. 'Too little too late' cried the consumer organisations.

Products do fail. Packaging does go wrong. There is nothing new about problems with products but these days a product problem can rapidly escalate to a crisis. Retailers and manufacturers have always been aware of the need to provide the purchaser with products that are reliable. Even going back to the days of products being sold off the back of a horse-drawn cart, if goods failed badly, then that hawker was not allowed back in the town unless he replaced the goods.

There was the classic case, *Donohue* v. *Stevenson* (1932), which identified that a member of the public could bring an action in negligence against the manufacturer of goods that created a problem. The product was ginger beer which had been sold to the owner of a Glasgow café. The café sold this ginger beer to a shop assistant's lady friend. When pouring a glass of the product, a decomposed snail arrived in the glass. The young woman became quite ill and suffered considerable fright from the horror of seeing the snail. She sued for damages. She claimed the manufacturer was negligent in letting the snail crawl into the bottle during manufacturing process.

The British House of Lords expressed the view that the manufacturers owed a duty of care for the bottle not to contain anything that might be poisonous or harmful. A manufacturer of food, medicine or a similar article, who sold these in circumstances where the distributor or consumer could not discover any defect on a reasonable inspection (in this case the bottle was opaque and sealed by a metal press cap) was under a legal duty to the ultimate consumer or purchaser to take reasonable care that the article was free from any defect likely to cause injury. The plaintiff won 100 pounds compensation from the manufacturer.

In Europe, the United States and Australia today, governments have introduced a strict liability regime under which anyone injured by defective goods can sue the manufacturer or the importer without having to prove negligence or breach of contract or warranty. In deciding whether goods are defective, consideration is given to the manner in which they have been marketed, their packaging, labelling, instructions and the date of manufacturer.

Whether it is a food scare, or a design defect, a health problem, a manufacturing error, criminal tampering or injury, defective product management and product recall is part of the manufacturing process. One of the most critical elements that is faced in every product problem is the ability of the manufacturer or maker to realise the point at which the problem can escalate to a crisis status. As soon as a manufacturer pulls a product off the shelves or out of the showroom, the alarm bells begin to ring. Is it just a safety check or minor issue or could it develop into a serious problem?

Most standard product recall plans call for a series of actions which stop the distribution of the problem product and future sales, retrieving any problem products as well as notifying the public about what has happened.

You only have to look in most of the consumer magazines to find a list of product recalls. Daily newspapers carry small advertisements advising that a product will be recalled and detailing its batch number, its name and description, the nature of the problem and so on.

And with every problem comes the possibility that the company involved could face a class action. Societies are becoming increasingly litigation-conscious. Product liability cases continue to generate huge media coverage.

In the United States, the intrauterine birth control device, the Dalkon shield, manufactured by A. H. Robbins, had its sales suspended after a study linked the device to pelvic inflammatory diseases resulting in spontaneous abortions. Later the company went into bankruptcy.

*Fortune Magazine* made the following reference to the litigation process relative to cases such as the Dow Corning silicone breast implant case.

"It usually begins slowly, almost imperceptibly, the first faint gust of wind that signals the coming storm. Somewhere in America, a plaintiff's lawyer files a lawsuit alleging that a familiar and widely used product harmed his client. Then, somewhere else, a second plaintiff's lawyer files a similar suit. A third is filed, then a fourth, until there are dozens of parallel 'tort' claims across the country, all making the same accusation about the same product.

"Yet as long as these remain individual suits in individual jurisdictions, crawling a long at their own pace, they don't necessarily pose a mortal threat to the product's manufacturer.

"They have no broader context, no larger meaning. Which is to say, the perception has not yet taken hold among the nation's plaintiffs lawyers that there is in these cases—or more precisely, in the *accumulation* of these cases—a tremendous opportunity to bring a company down, and to make a killing in the process."

(Joseph Nocera, *Fortune Magazine*, 16 October 1995.)

In 1994 the Dow Corning silicone breast implant case attracted enormous media coverage. Women who had breast implants complained they were having serious problems, which were attributed to the implant.

It was front-page news and a feature of every investigative media program in the United States. The company went into denial. As far as managing the crisis—the message agenda had been led for far too long by journalists, special interest groups and medical commentators often lacking solid scientific evidence. The subject was one of extreme sensitivity with horrific photographs and stories appearing in women's magazines. The government called for a moratorium on implant use. Defendants agreed to a US$4.25 billion 'global settlement' for 480 000 claimants. Dow Corning filed for bankruptcy.

Gun makers in the United States are in the midst of a crisis. Over 100 cities are set to file lawsuits looking for billions of dollars of compensation from gun makers related to crimes where guns have caused death or injury. The famous gun company, Smith & Wesson, are developing crisis plans to shield assets and reputation should huge judgments be awarded against it. More than 35 000 Americans die and many more are seriously injured in crimes with guns each year, according to the US National Centre for Health Statistics. The suggestion is that these lawsuits against gunmakers are inspired by the success of the billions of dollars in settlements from the tobacco industry for patients who have suffered smoking-related illnesses.

At the heart of any product crisis, is how early the problem or threat is identified. These days, that threat is increasingly related to litigation and class action. Just like any threat, the effects of such litigation have to be brainstormed, working with lawyers, to identify well in advance the worse case scenario.

If you have a product that in some way can cause harm, what will happen? And it is worth not just thinking about the small cases that could hit your business, but what about sequential problems? The cases we have talked about so far were caused by a number of events escalating.

A crisis team needs to work with issues managers, product development managers, marketing managers, researchers and technologists to determine the effects of possible legal action related to manufacturing errors, contamination, defects, allergies or injuries caused by using the product. It is planning ahead for the possibility that will protect your market and maintain your brand reputation and business continuity.

## SEQUENTIAL PROBLEMS ESCALATE

When the carcinogen benzine was found in the world famous Perrier water in 1994, the company responded in various ways in different parts of the world, but certainly the Perrier brand was damaged because of the mixed response from various parts of the organisation. Sales slumped.

Intel, the world leader in microchips, was slow to respond when it found a product problem in its Pentium microprocessors in 1994. An academic customer, working on a research project, identified difficulties with calculations. He contacted Intel, who informed him that they had many reports of the problem but it did not warrant a product recall. So, he e-mailed his associates regarding the problem and as a result of this Internet discussion of the problem, there were further requests to Intel from more customers. The audience grew larger and included a number of specialist computer reporters, including Steve Young, from CNN, who reported on technology. The bug story was picked up from CNN by a number of other media, including the *New York Times*. The Internet was now buzzing with stories about the problem. Intel was offering new chips to high-end users but they had to justify that they needed one for special use.

Then, as the problem continued to escalate, and the computer public roared with concern, IBM stopped shipments of its Pentium-equipped personal computers. This IBM decision hit the media front pages and current affairs programs worldwide. Pentium-equipped computers were given the thumbs down by the experts.

The Internet had been at the forefront of an industry-wide reputational crisis for Intel and much of the debate from both the consumer and the industry had been conducted through e-mail and the Internet. Certainly part of the new approach to accountability and *vox populi*.

Crisis management was not triggered early enough. Much of the customer outrage could have been dealt with through early identification of the seriousness of an emerging product problem and, subsequently, the closer attention to growing customer dissatisfaction. The crisis escalated through the consumers spreading the message on the very technology that lay at the heart of the problem.

The company Phillip Morris USA initially dealt very efficiently with a cigarette recall in 1995. The contamination affected a small part of a batch of about three billion cigarettes. Phillip Morris recalled eight billion cigarettes and provided details of the possible effect of the contaminant. They outlined effects such as coughing, wheezing and eye irritation. Their help line was set up immediately and they reviewed their production methods to make sure the situation could not happen again. A dedicated group of employees was given the task of recalling and replacing the affected cigarettes.

The Chief Executive of Phillip Morris USA, James Morgan, stated that the contamination was identified on 19 May, which was a week before Phillip Morris made its public statement about the problem. The fact that they announced the recall just before a long weekend has been identified by some commentators as an attempt to reduce media coverage of the problem.

The blame factor became an issue. Just as Perrier blamed their bottling line cleaning fluid for the benzine in their bubbles, when in fact it was the filters at the spring that were the problem, so Phillip Morris blamed the company Hoescht Celanese. Phillip Morris suggested that the contaminant in its cigarettes was caused by a plasticiser spray used in the making of the filter. Hoescht did not accept the blame stating that all its products and processes were within specification. The argument escalated an issue to a crisis for both organisations. The argument gave the media an opportunity to create an atmosphere of blame.

There is a tendency in the product recall roundabout for well-known brand product manufacturers to blame suppliers or packaging processes for problems. This tends to come back to haunt the company and the brand if the blame cannot be substantiated.

In all product recall planning, an organisation must consider its public responsibility, its corporate responsibility and its ongoing market imperative of protecting the brand and the market share. (See Figure 10.1)

# RECALL PROCEDURES

In every business, consumer product recalls will have a different requirement. It is no overstatement to suggest that in some cases, these product recalls may be a matter of life and death. In all cases, retrieving a product as well as notifying the public, involves fast and efficient processes.

The following is a plan that covers the general guidelines on what to do when faced with a product recall, particularly related to the complexity of modern processes associated with manufacturing, storage and distribution (see Figure 10.2). The crisis trigger forms part of this plan.

## Step 1—Product problem

Establishing an early warning system to identify the vulnerability related to product recall is the starting point of any recall plan. The field of threats may cover signals from the production line that there are defects in the product or manufacturing areas.

174

**Figure 10.1** *Product recall corporate social responsibilities*

---

### The Public Responsibility

• To prevent consumers suffering injury, death or damage.

• To comply with all laws and regulations.

### The Responsibility to Shareholders

• To protect the assets and earnings of the company.

• To manage risk and compliance.

• To ensure business continuation and recovery.

### The Marketing Imperative

• To protect/recover the brand.

• To retain and recover market share.

• To protect/recover corporate reputation.

---

There is the threat that packaging may be inferior or labelling of information incorrect. The product may have problems related to safety standards. Weather may have had an effect on the product in its transportation or distribution. The product may have been tampered with or may have been subject to some criminal contamination.

Your line of contact can come from signals from within the organisation at manufacturing or marketing level, or may well come from salespeople in the field. Outside, your customers may be the signal and consumer complaints could well come from anywhere in the market. You may also get information about a product problem from a retailer, or manufacturer, government or regulatory organisation.

If the product has been tampered with or is the subject of extortion, you may be contacted by law enforcement agencies. The other signal may come from the media, either as a complaint or concern from a consumer via radio or television talk programs or via a story or editorial in a newspaper or magazine. Whatever the source, your product problem signal must efficiently reach your senior management group and recall co-ordinator.

*Figure 10.2* The product recall flow chart

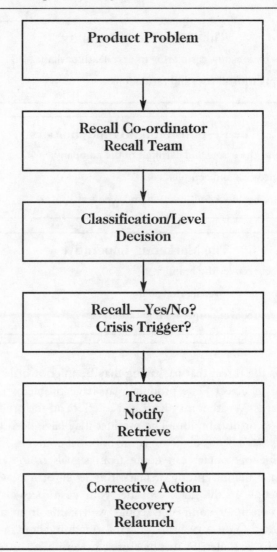

### Step 2—Product recall co-ordinator and product recall team

When a product problem hits, the role of the Product Recall Co-ordinator and the product recall team is critical. Certainly, the CEO should be contacted and at least given a clear picture of the threats involved.

If there is any chance of the threat escalating to affect the future of the organisation, then the CEO needs to be advised and the crisis team should be called out in addition to the product recall team. If it is just a standard recall, then the product recall team can do their job and achieve the process efficiently.

The recall team should consist of the Recall Co-ordinator, Senior Production Manager, Distribution Manager, Communications or Public Relations Manager, and a Marketing Manager. Supporting these roles should be the Risk, Legal Services and Human Resources Managers.

## Step 3—Classification/level decision

A severity matrix should be drawn up to classify each level of risk. Once the classification has been identified in terms of its severity, then the level of recall can be identified. The Recall Co-ordinator will then make the decision (often in consultation with the CEO) accordingly.

## Step 4—Recall – yes/no?

If the recall decision is no, then the Recall Co-ordinator may decide to continue to manage the problem with a small team. It will be necessary to continually collect information needed to assess the situation and to keep in touch with the complaint or problem source and affected stakeholders. Certainly, a continual review of consumer, retailer and distributor feedback will be essential and it may be necessary to conduct a communications program with the customer.

If the decision is yes, then formal notification or initiation of the recall will need to be carried out. The government will need to be contacted and the reason and details of the recall stated. The organisation will need to comply with government regulations regarding all relevant information related to the product batch, quantity and the type of problem and assessment of the threat with the proposed actions.

Preparations will need to be made internally to brief employees and to deal with inquiries related to the product and its traceability. Hot lines may need to be established and preparation for media inquiries set up.

It is at this point that the decision to activate the full crisis management plan should be made. Could the actions that are about to take place (either yes or no) cause a public response that may affect the company's well-being? The crisis team leader needs to identify the threats at crisis level and evaluate the impact across the organisation.

It is time here to respond to the large number of inquiries from customers, employees, distributors, academics, government and the media. It is time for the crisis management team to back-up the product recall team to deal with a very large number of inquiries or negative comments. Additional telephone systems may be required. The CEO and senior management need to be briefed for interviews. Financial audiences will need to be addressed. The crisis team will need to decide at this point who the spokesperson will be and at what stage the CEO may be required to lead the message strategy. (See Chapter 6–Communicating Actions.)

## Step 5—Trace, notify and retrieve

Initial recall notification can be made by telephone, supported by e-mail, facsimile or letter, usually no later than 48 hours after the start of the recall. The recall notification in certain cases may require a personal visit by staff because of the sensitive nature of the product or problem. If the recall moves to the retailer or the consumer, then advertisements may be necessary in print media, or if the matter is urgent and serious, it may, in addition, be considered necessary to recall through the medium of television or radio.

The product will be returned to a central location for audit and review and consideration made at this point for controlled and audited destruction. Security is an important factor here—additional support from an outside security organisation may be required to ensure and safeguard returned or damaged products. The way in which the organisation deals with a product defect will dictate the way in which the consumer or the retailer is reimbursed or compensated. Importantly, the product has to be traced efficiently through its channels of distribution.

If a crisis has been declared, this is the stage where the crisis team could well be subject to an enormous number of calls from major customers and the general public. The work of the crisis team will be very much into containment of reputation and damage limitation to the business.

## Step 6—Corrective action, recovery, relaunch

Corrective action includes all the activities required to confirm that consumers, distributors and retailers have been effectively covered in the response and that the product recall has been complete, i.e. the product returned to its source. There should be confirmation that there are no unsafe products still in the marketplace. All stakeholders should be checked to ensure that messages have been received. An audit trail should be confirmed on the notification process and the products returned.

Short-term and long-term recovery objectives need to be set to achieve continuing protection of the consumer and maintain market share. Market research may be required to identify the problems associated with the product recall and product image. Consideration needs to be given to issues such as redesign, relabel and redevelopment of the product or its packaging. It may be necessary to increase contact with customers and repair any damage to the corporate image or reputation of the brand.

The company may have to deal with investigations, litigation and a review of safety standards over a long period. There may even be international issues that have to be dealt with through planned government or public relations programs.

In extreme cases, a product recall may lead to a complete product relaunch. This will mean a review of the pricing, branding and packaging of the product. It could well consider a restructuring of wholesaling, transportation and warehousing and to complete the marketing integration process, a campaign relaunch including advertising, sales promotion and public relations.

# A YEAR IN THE LIFE OF PRODUCT RECALL

In reviewing product recall response and effect in one country over a 12-month period, the author has looked at the management of the problem of product recall in the food industry and protection of the consumer as well as business continuity. The country is Australia with a population of 18.5 million. Media coverage of food-related crises and product recall amongst the highest in the country's history during the 1996–97 period were:

- 23 April: Orange juice from Sandhurst Farms is recalled due to metal fragments being found inside the bottle.
- 21 May: Nineteen of 23 plaintiffs in a case relating to Garibaldi Smallgoods (sausages) are paid up to A$10 million compensation. (As a result of eating the contaminated sausage, one girl died and 24 people were hospitalised.) Processed meat sales dropped throughout Australia. Garibaldi goes out of business.
- 17 June: Mercury is found in some tubs of the top-selling brand Streets Ice Cream. Major product recall follows.
- 23 June: General Foods recalls nine brands of peanut butter including top brand, Kraft (70% of the peanut butter market). One man dies, 54 people contract salmonella gastroenteritis. Problem traced to Peanut Company of Australia, Queensland supplier to Kraft. Mouse faeces blamed for salmonella problem.

179

- 26 June: Kraft has total recall of peanut butter. The recall cost is estimated at A$55 million.
- 28 June: Muesli candy bars are withdrawn by General Foods. They contain peanut butter and are related to scare.
- 9 July: On behalf of seven applicants, Australian law firm, Slater and Gordon, files claim against Kraft Foods.
- 19 August: In class action, Slater and Gordon, has 640 persons suing Kraft and General Foods.
- 4 November: Three hundred and forty-eight passengers on 14 Qantas flights from Cairns to Japan suffer food poisoning from chocolate sauce made in Cairns.
- 29 November: Australia's largest retail store, Myer Grace Bros, closes one of its restaurants after 24 people suffer food poisoning from suspect sandwiches. Myer moves quickly to review standards.
- 17 December: Mrs Mary McNamee, 92-years old, dies after eating hospital food infected by salmonella at Brisbane's Public Hospital. The infected hospital food poisons 26 other people.
- 3 February: An extortion letter is sent to a newspaper in Queensland and the Police Commissioner in New South Wales. Letter makes threats to poison Australia's top-selling Arnott's Biscuits.
- 14 February: Arnott's Biscuits removed from all the southern and eastern states of Australia.
- 15 February: Oyster scare. A man dies from eating oysters originating from New South Wales. Confirmed hepatitis infection. One hundred and fifty other people contract Hepatitis A.
- 22 February: Recall of three processed meat products by Lago Smallgoods. Two people died and 30 people contract gastroenteritis and are poisoned by salmonella muechen bacteria.
- 26 February: Police and Arnott's announce situation safe. Supermarkets and shops are restocked with Arnott's biscuits and advertising programs launched.
- 24 March: Headline news. Hot bread shop causes 50 people illness from salmonella food poisoning after serving pork rolls. People affected increases to 554.
- 27 March: One person dies of salmonella poisoning from pork rolls. Hot bread shop closed.
- 2 April: Don Smallgoods, makers of processed meat products, recalls products after salmonella bacteria is found in liverwurst and cabanossi. On same day, Fabbris Processed Meats recalls ham products in three states after 19 people become ill.

- 7 April: Safeway Deli closed when warning given by health authorities related to salmonella. Sausages recalled.
- 10 April: General Foods Kraft offers plaintiffs compensation payments but must register as part of class action by mid-August.
- 14 April: Thirty people ill after eating chicken curry. Five hospitalised. Bottles of Meadow Vale cream recalled following glass fragments scare.

Source: Walker, David M., *The Age*, 19 April, 1997.

## DELIBERATE TAMPERING

The landmark case of the Tylenol tampering in the United States is still the ultimate textbook study in product recall crisis management. Tylenol's maker, Johnson & Johnson's, capability of working with the Food and Drug Administration and instigating a total recall and then a total relaunch set an unprecedented standard. Many companies have followed the example.

Deliberate tampering can be categorised into two areas. The first is basically petty pilfering and the second extortion, hoaxes and counterfeiting.

Petty crimes of pilfering and interference with products or packaging in the showroom or on the shelf costs manufacturers and industry dearly. The security issues related to label damage, seal breaking and damaged products is increasing in most businesses. How many of us have looked at supermarket shoppers opening a lid and tasting the product before buying it? The health and safety problems related to this are enormous.

The second problem is extortion, hoaxes and counterfeiting, and carries with it a product recall of crisis proportions. Food tampering of any kind eventually becomes a police investigation. Deliberate contamination, or threats to a product that might injure or kill, is a serious crime. Unfortunately, just as kidnap and ransom can be used to manipulate the media for political or personal gain, so too can extortion related to food products.

Often these threats lead to a withdrawal or recall of the product from the shelves. It is a time when the product recall team has to work closely with the company crisis management team and law enforcement agencies.

Deliberate product tampering has quite a different response than a contamination caused by temperature change or time.

In accidental contamination or product damage, microbiological diagnostic assistance or technological research can usually track down the problem, and the product recall becomes a severe issue of reputation damage. It can often lead to the demise of the organisation.

In the case of deliberate tampering and extortion, while there could well be a loss of sales and business, the public are much more understanding about the problem and, in most cases, if the communication process is sufficient, the organisation and brand will recover their market over time.

Tampering with baby food was a major crisis for Heinz in the United Kingdom a decade ago and led to the destruction of 100 million jars of baby food valued at around A$100 million, as a result of a contamination scare of splinters of glass. The contamination was an extortion issue and the police had proposed to the crisis management committee that no information should be given to the media, while they were attempting to capture the criminal. They were unsuccessful in their plan and eventually the police issued information on the blackmailer. Shrink-wrapped packaging was proposed by the crisis management committee but the police had been running the agenda.

The criminal had also planted poison in other products and made threats about using cyanide and other lethal poison. He was finally caught but it took time due to his inside knowledge of police operations and it turned out he was an ex-detective with considerable access to police operational planning.

As a result of this extortion case, Heinz and a number of other organisations repackaged their products with new security devices including a safety button showing whether the seal has been broken and a plastic, overall shrink-wrap.

Tamper-evident packaging is becoming an international standard. While consumers can never be entirely sure whether the product has been interfered with, manufacturers need to take the best possible approach to protecting their valuable market and brand. One of the most serious problems related to product extortion is the fact that the crime can demand the immediate involvement of senior police and government officials. The law enforcement officers will usually take full control and the company and the product brand can, through these circumstances, be pushed unintentionally into the background.

In the Tylenol case, Johnson & Johnson acted ahead of the government agenda and took the communication high ground. In the case of the Heinz Baby Food tampering case in the United Kingdom, Scotland Yard ran the agenda and caused the company to take a back row position, thus affecting the brand and the recovery.

Sorting out who will run the agenda, and how it will be run, is something that has to be done in advance when it comes to a serious case of extortion. There has to be a clear understanding about the company's role and communication capability with the law enforcement organisation involved. The most efficient way to be sure this will work is to establish lines of communication with the law enforcement agency before anything happens. Decide on how the organisation will work with the senior police and government officials. Not only will this help to cut away the bureaucratic barriers, but it will also help to give a more combined response to the problem.

There is nothing worse in a product tampering extortion situation than to see the CEO of a major international company sitting in the back row behind the Chief of Police when the statement being made by the Chief relates to the future of the brand and the parent company concerned. It is vital for a company to work at being part of the communication strategy during a crisis of this nature.

Integrate product recall planning with crisis planning and involve law enforcement agencies in your planning. Have regular product recall and crisis exercises to test various kinds of product threats.

# CONTROL POINTS

- ☐ These days, a product problem can rapidly escalate to crisis.

- ☐ With every product problem, comes the possibility of a class action.

- ☐ Crisis teams need to work with issues managers, product development managers, marketing managers, researchers and technologists to determine threats.

- ☐ Consideration needs to be given to manufacturing errors, contamination, defects, allergies or injuries caused by using the product.

- ☐ Product recall processes must include a crisis trigger.

- ☐ Establish an early warning system to identify the vulnerability related to product recall.

- ☐ In extreme cases of a product crisis, recovery may involve a product relaunch or repackaging.

- ☐ Extortion, hoaxes and counterfeiting related to products are generally product recalls of crisis proportions.

- ☐ Deliberate contamination or threats to a product that might injure or kill are crises that require the involvement of law enforcement agencies.

- ☐ Run regular product recall and integrated crisis exercises to test various kinds of product threats.

# 11

## REHEARSING THE PLAN

The huge chimney was one of the tallest edifices in the country town. It represented the height and success of this industry's plant operations. The manufacturing operations that spread out below it were numerous, and the thousands of employees working around the clock relied on this thriving operation for continued employment. Now, the problems of pollution had been reduced by new, scientifically developed processes that successfully stabilised the omissions and provided a much healthier environment for the surrounding town dwellers. The large Bell Jet Ranger helicopter team that serviced the top of the stack were experienced in making technical adjustments. But this day the wind was at twice its strength. Suddenly, the giant blades of the helicopter sliced into the concrete of the chimney, sending the spinning machine crashing into the many buildings and tanks below and setting off a diesel fuel fireball. The crisis and emergency teams were on call immediately. This was only an exercise but the teams were ready to deal with the problem because they were trained up for an event such as this.

There are countless files of costly crisis management, risk management, emergency management, issues management and product recall plans that sit gathering dust on corporate shelves. They are simply no use unless the people using them are trained and tested. Crisis-prone organisations are exposed and vulnerable without a process that assures continual review and testing of plans.

It is not just organisations involved in oil, resources, transport or manufacturing who need to train up for crisis management. Organisations operating in hazardous industries invariably have and test crisis plans, but it is amazing how many organisations in the service sector, such as banking and finance, legal and accounting, who have never tested a plan or a team.

A large legal firm recently had cause to face its own internal crisis with the rapid departure of a number of senior partners following an issue of ethics. Countless media arrived in the plush foyer of that legal firm and the crisis lingered for many weeks. There may have been a crisis plan in place but very few of the senior management partners had ever practised their response to such a situation. Damage control took far too long and their client base was seriously affected by the loss of reputation.

In order for any organisation to respond rapidly, it needs to continually train its teams in strategies for response, damage limitation and recovery. Crisis management training involves the education and testing of the CORE team and additional specialist education for divisional and location teams. Training introduces the process of crisis management to the teams and allows them to work through typical scenarios based on crisis threats. Once individual team role players have worked through a number of typical events, they will have a far better understanding of what strategies are needed for managing a crisis when it occurs.

The *Titanic* was the ship with everything from stem to stern, including emergency plans. But the plans were never tested, nor were the lifeboats. When more than 1500 people died, the world was rightfully stunned by this massive maritime disaster. As a result of the *Titanic* sinking, the UK Board of Trade introduced new regulations which meant that in future ships would test their emergency plans to a far greater extent and that ships would have sufficient lifeboats to deal with mass evacuation.

The lessons about testing plans seem to travel the world with the crises through time. In more recent years, Occidental Petroleum Company, too, had emergency plans. But when the Piper Alpha disaster struck and their oil production platform at sea blew up killing 167 men, the systems for control proved seriously ineffective and work practices judged unsafe. There were obviously gaps in the planning, and worst case scenarios were not prepared for. Underestimating the nature of the threat meant that when the disaster hit, the whole safety system failed. The report stated: 'They failed to ensure emergency training was being provided as intended. The platform personnel and management were not prepared for a major emergency as they should have been.'

Again, when the Air Florida 737 aeroplane crashed into the freezing Potomac River in 1982, emergency response teams and plans were rendered ineffective by the teams' inability to quickly reach and retrieve the survivors struggling in the ice-bound water. The plans had not catered for this worst case weather scenario.

Once the crisis management plan and manual is completed, the immediate requirement is to ensure the training of teams and the testing of plans. This is done by conducting crisis discussion groups, think-tanks and response drills. The most effective way to review the plan is to simulate a crisis situation and have the response carried out in a realistic way.

It is important that the CEO and senior management approve a consistent program of training. Dedicated resources, money and effort are needed to assure that management personnel and employee teams are given the highest possible education and certification to effectively perform their jobs. Where possible, the training standards should be set by a qualified facilitator to ensure course competency and an auditing process.

The biggest problem faced by crisis management leaders will be the difficulty in getting team members together to train and practise. The most successful plans are those that make sure the team rehearses as a unit. Where the CEO is available for the head office team training process, the organisation can be assured of a successful and committed result. This involvement will be a great team builder and incentive across the organisation.

A schedule and critical path need to be set out for the training plan. Objectives, facilitation and materials required need to be identified. Evaluation of performance criteria should be confirmed.

The components of a training presentation will require materials such as overheads, software, handouts, and notes. As a general rule, slides and overheads can be used to present the agenda and demonstrate the system. Flow charts and key actions can be listed. Some organisations transfer these charts and actions to appropriate software for ease of transport.

Where should the training take place? Crisis management training and, in particular, workshops and exercises, should take place at the location of the team. Just as it is mandatory to regularly test the capability of emergency equipment at any location, so it should be as important to test the team at the location. A crisis plan is only as good as its application to the organisation and location it is written for.

Conducting a training program far away from an office, location or site does not provide the most efficient result. Crisis threats need to be put into context with the location. People relate more to workshopping vulnerabilities when they are close to the location where the events may happen.

Crisis management training that uses a mock control centre with hot and cold running technology and well-designed operations rooms is counterpoint to efficient instruction, simulation or testing response performance.

Teams need to be confronted by their own 'hands-on' working model, so they can identify with the problems and opportunities of their surroundings. This way, they will identify the gaps in terms of human and technical resources and better relate to the difficulties they will have to face in a real response situation. Telephones will not work properly, tables will be too small, power sources will overload, rooms will get too hot, toilets will be too far away and security will break down—these are the sorts of things that do happen in the real world and are a vital part of testing people and equipment in a crisis training program.

A schedule of training times should be confirmed 12 months in advance. This schedule should indicate a process for completing a workshop first, followed by a desk-top exercise where the team confronts a possible crisis. This is followed by a full-scale exercise where the team is given a virtual reality event to control. Confirmation of who will be trained and how they will be evaluated needs to be included in the documentation.

Training must include crisis management overview sessions for employee support teams, contractors and other outside suppliers who may be involved in the crisis response.

## THE CRISIS WORKSHOP—
## DISCUSSIONS AND THINK-TANKS

The workshop is the essential starting point and introduction for the team to the plan. Essentially, the training is aimed at members of the CORE team. The team can be made up of the team leader, human resources and family co-ordinator, emergency services and security co-ordinator, operations co-ordinator, control room and call-out co-ordinator, administration and commercial services co-ordinator and the recovery co-ordinator. This is an example of a typical team structure that could make up the CORE team.

Each team member's role should represent his or her line management area. This way, the team co-ordinators will understand how their specialist skills will be applied to the crisis response. As emphasised in Chapter 3, the plan is based on what the team does before, during and after a crisis. The 'before' stage identifies what each team member does to prepare for or avoid a crisis.

If, for example, the threat was air transport at a difficult location, perhaps new travel procedures requiring improved standards of aircraft could be considered. In the case of chemical spills, greater safety procedures and improved storage facilities may be put in place at the container area.

The workshop should show participants that some crises are not preventable and tend to give little or no warning. These include product tampering, hostile takeovers, explosions or natural disasters. However, there is a lot that can be done in early planning for a response to these threats.

The 'during' and 'after' stages for each role will be worked through, so that each team member understands what to do when a crisis hits and how to commence the process of recovery.

Team members need to be backed up. Ideally, each of these team roles should have two alternatives. These alternatives should attend the workshop at the same time. Separate workshops can be organised for support and administration teams.

The workshop should identify how crisis management is linked to the organisational business strategy. The threat analysis of vulnerabilities should lead to group discussion and team contribution of creative ways of dealing with the problem. Team members and their alternatives should be encouraged to also consider unintended consequences that may occur as a result of the crisis.

For example, if the workshop was identifying product tampering as a key threat, then the problem should be considered in terms of product recall, not just locally but countrywide. The escalation of the problem could emphasise the effects on the organisation if the product caused serious injury or even death. Legal issues such as class action could be factored in.

If the threat identified in the workshop was a serious accident at a plant or operation, then the workshop attendees should be encouraged to think about what would happen if outside assistance became impossible because of a road blockage or bad weather. They should consider what would happen if there was not sufficient medical assistance available in the early stages of the response to deal with the victims of the incident.

In all crisis management workshop discussions, the worst possible scenario needs to be brought into focus. What would happen if the CEO was not available as a spokesperson? What would happen if there was a similar incident at another business nearby at the same time?

In fact, the team should be asked to consider what would happen if they were unavailable—how would alternatives be brought in? What would happen if the operations room in which the team was working was cut off or rendered unworkable?

These workshop discussions and think-tanks, based on crisis threats, assist in improving not only the crisis management plan but also developing the technical support systems required should the crisis occur.

Ultimately, the best test for the crisis management team will be to perform their roles in an active simulation, but brainstorming the threats and reviewing past problems provides a very strong understanding of how crisis affects the total organisation. It is when the group determines the effects of each vulnerability on the business that they will understand how their crisis management role and responsibility is relevant 'before', 'during' and 'after' a crisis.

A warning. Workshops should not spend hours on reviewing emergency response techniques, public relations strategies or security tactics. The principal purpose of these workshops is to look at managing the corporate implications of a crisis. Fighting the fire, controlling the crowds, dealing with leaking chemicals or sorting out the arrival of journalists is not the purpose of the CORE team. This is a training program for managers on how to make on-the-spot decisions that will assist in securing business continuity and protecting the future.

The workshop needs a strict agenda. The following sample covers many of the subjects in a typical crisis workshop.

## Standard crisis management workshop agenda

Objective: to provide a management workshop that will enable crisis management team members to understand the basic principals of crisis management and its application within the organisation. The program is designed to review the crisis management plan, team roles and responsibilities, threats and responses.

- Crisis training objectives: what the session will achieve.
- Introduction to crisis—cause and effects: definitions and examples.

- Crisis prevention and warning systems: actions to prevent crises.
- The value of crisis management: the benefits of being ready—strategies for damage control.
- Overview of the plan and manual: walk through each element of the plan and clarify.
- Crisis management team—roles and responsibilities: what each role means and what that team member has to do.
- Threat analysis: where is the organisation vulnerable and what are the possible effects on the business?
- Review response strategies: work through checklists of response actions for each threat.
- Integration with outside resources: review plans with emergency services, police, security, state disaster organisations, etc.
- Discuss how to communicate best with stakeholders, employees, customers, media, community, etc.
- Technology and equipment and location: where does the crisis team meet and what essential technology and equipment do they need?
- Log keeping and documentation: confirm document control and efficiency program for retaining information.
- Test and evaluate: using typical threat, team provides discussion on how they would respond to the crisis using the examples and lessons learnt.

Case studies of past crises provide important insights, background and experience. They give the team an opportunity to observe the way in which past crises have been handled, at the same time as evaluating how recovery was instigated.

The workshop in most cases will be first conducted at the organisation's head office with the CORE team. As with all the training units in the crisis management plan, it should then be transferred to regional and divisional business units, operations and sites. In some cases at smaller sites, the workshop may involve teams of two or three people, but they can still carry out threat identification and the responses to their unique situation.

## THE DESK-TOP EXERCISE

Once the initial education program has been completed and teams are aware of the crisis management planning process and response, the next stage is to test the plans by conducting a crisis response drill. This is where a crisis event is simulated and the team responds as realistically as possible. The transfer of knowledge about the plan and the team's functions can be tested in a very face-to-face way.

The desk-top exercise provides a means for teams to actually deal head-on with a crisis situation and to quickly identify areas that can be improved. Leadership and negotiation now come into play as the emphasis is put on the individual ability of team members to anticipate the needs of their stakeholders and effectively co-ordinate responses against a background of urgency and confusion.

Now the team becomes an action group. The leader must take control and brief his or her team about the problem and the direction. The objective is to build strong, flexible and versatile thinking. Without doubt, after just one desk-top exercise, team members are infinitely better prepared for dealing with a serious situation. At the same time they become more receptive to the plan and its place in the organisation.

The desk-top exercise is a pre-emptor for the bigger event, the full-scale exercise. It sets up and familiarises team members with the way in which their fellow team members cope with the demands related to the response. For example, the team will have to deal with many communication streams at the one time. The human resources co-ordinator will need to get the message out to employees at the same time as the public affairs co-ordinator is shaping the first message for the media and consequently the other audiences.

This session shows the team how information about a problem is received in the control room and how it is disseminated to the outside world. Most of all, the exercise will create a pressure point to put the team in a state of realisation about the importance of their decision-making process, resource allocation and task co-ordination.

Exercises should happen a number of times a year to give the team a chance to face a wide variety of exercise responses. They should be given the chance to respond as a crisis team to the threats of accidents, criminal events, ethical issues, environmental spills, cases of sexual harassment, bad weather and so on.

## Setting up and preparing the desk-top exercise

If the facilitator of the desk-top exercise spends sufficient time preparing the background material, presentation notes, scenario structure and handouts, then the desk-top exercise will have realistic value in improving decision-making skills. Organisations may choose to do this exercise preparation themselves or could employ a consultant who is experienced in exercise development and production. Either way, a quality standard should be set for the running of the exercise so that time spent by team members, executives and personnel is perceived as valuable and important. This, after all, is a starting point for a long-term quality commitment.

Laying the groundwork for the exercise involves a number of tasks which will require some input from various areas of the organisation including human resources, operational management, emergency services, product research and finance.

Scripting the desk-top scenario is not unlike writing the storyline for a play. The scenario has to be written in a number of parts. In the theatre, a rehearsal gives the director and actors an opportunity to experience the entire theatrical presentation; to work together as an ensemble and to make necessary adjustments to their performance. This is the same in desk-top exercises. The team have to perform their roles. Your scenario will set the scene. A good desk-top exercise should last between 60 and 90 minutes. It should be well-researched and challenge the team so they can find ways of keeping the organisation strong in times of trouble.

## Task No. 1—Research it

Discuss with management (not the team) the most likely threats asking 'What is our worst threat?'. Confirm the threat you are going to use for the desk-top exercise and then add additional 'things that could go wrong' within this threat exposure. Now you are ready to write your desk-top exercise scenario.

## Task No. 2—Write it

Prepare your scenario in five or six parts thinking all the time about it being read by the team and how they will work to take control of the crisis situation. Keep the scenario fairly brief and do not overdramatise the situation. You can work in 'real' time, which is as the incidents would happen, or in 'compressed' time, which is taking an event that may happen over two days, back into say one hour. Test out the scenario on one of the senior executives, so that it has clout and is current.

## Task No. 3—Add calls

From your research, now identify four to six stakeholders who would respond to a crisis at each level of the simulation. For example, if the simulation was a fire and explosion, then in the first or second part of the simulation, calls would come in from employees' families, neighbours, your own people, customers, government and, of course, the media. List your stakeholder calls in a second list.

## Task No. 4—Brief the team

Set out the key objectives and briefing notes in order to brief your team. Detail the criteria that you are going to use to review their performance, i.e. how the team performed as a whole, how individual roles were performed, etc.

## Task No. 5—Locate the room

Identify the room in which the desk-top exercise will take place. Make sure it is equipped with a whiteboard and telephones. Make sure you have given the team a call register and an incident form in order for them to fill out their actions as they work through the problem.

## Task No. 6—Secure it

Any exercise, desk-top or full-scale, requires an element of sensitivity. Written documents of dreadful events related to a company can be fodder for the media in real terms and should be given security status in its preparation and use. Limit the number of copies of the scenario and prepare the documents with a statement such as: 'This is an exercise for training purposes only.'

## Task No. 7—Run the exercise

Now you are ready to run your desk-top exercise and test the team. A word of warning. Do not turn this into a media crisis exercise. While it is very exciting to present pieces of paper to a group of people advising them that the media is knocking at every door and your favourite journalists are waiting with camera crews to attack. In the real world the media will only be a part of the crisis management team's responsibility. Certainly, the media may be responsible for the escalation of the event, but they are only one of the many audiences who will be a problem for the team. The unions may be demanding a more effective response, the chairperson of the organisation may be calling for answers and who knows, the Premier or the Prime Minister could be asking for explanations as to how the crisis happened.

Here are the key points to brief your team when they arrive in their meeting room or control room for their desk-top exercise:

•   As part of the ongoing crisis planning program for this organisation, today we are running a crisis desk-top exercise. The reasons for the desk-top exercise are to improve decision-making and team readiness at the same time as identifying any need for additional resources. We want each team member to involve themselves in the exercise. At the end of the scenario, we will debrief and integrate the lessons from today into our crisis management plan.

- You are located in the control room and you are a crisis management team for this organisation who have been called into this room to deal with a problem. You will be handed the scenario in six parts.

- Over the next 60–90 minutes, you should respond as a team to the problem and focus on managing the crisis in order to limit the damage to the organisation. Control the situation at the same time as communicating effectively with the necessary audiences. You should list your responses and the time of your actions on the whiteboard briefly as a log of events.

- Finally, you will receive from our imaginary switchboard a number of calls related to the crisis. Please register the calls and provide three or four words as to your suggested response. For example: 'We called back and advised the Mayor that we would give him a briefing at 4.00 p.m.' 'Told the journalist from CNN that we would give him a tour and interview at 3.00 p.m.'

| Item | Time | Event |
|------|------|-------|
| 1. | 7.00 p.m. | An explosion rocks the main building. You have emergency power. Rest of building is in darkness. Internal manager advises you that two floors have been destroyed, including all information technology. A number of people have been killed and injured. |
| 2. | 7.30 p.m. | Emergency services, police, fire, ambulances on-site. At this stage, nine people dead and 22 injured. Internal management reports extensive damage to all floors and major loss of information. Large group of customers were attending briefing meeting and drinks for the launch of a new product in presentation area. |
| 3. | 7.45 p.m. | Police and paramedics advise that two of the customers were killed and five others from the briefing meeting were seriously injured. A senior government minister has also been injured by the explosion. |

| Item | Time | Event |
|------|------|-------|
| 4. | 8.00 p.m. | Families of employees killed and injured in the blast and many other employees' families are making contact with the company. Telephone lines are limited. The media have set up a number of broadcast points outside the building and are reporting live. |
| 5. | 8.10 p.m. | Police advise that early investigations reveal that the explosion has been deliberate. A note is found referring to the organisation's unnecessary and unethical activities overseas. Police Chief announces to the media that this is the worst case of urban terrorism to a corporation in history. |
| 6. | 8.30 p.m. | An ex-employee walks into city police headquarters and gives himself up, admitting that he was responsible for the explosion. He had been fired five days ago and it appears that he was involved in part-time military service and had access to high explosives. |

## Desk-top exercise post-evaluation

After the exercise is declared completed, and the team members have had a chance to cool down, it will be time to debrief and review their performance. The facilitator should then make comments and lead the discussion of the overall crisis management response. Were they able to respond to the incident efficiently? What problems did they face? Could they get control of the situation early in the piece or did they feel it slipping away as the consequences changed? Did they use the plan and was it workable?

Once the overall response has been reviewed, then each team member should be given an overview of their individual response actions by the facilitator. Did they deal with their particular responsibilities effectively? What were the barriers that faced their roles and actions? Could their response have been handled better? What would help them perform their tasks better?

Finally, in summing up, the facilitator should comment on the leadership and interaction within the team. Lessons learnt from the desk-top exercise should be catalogued and added to the crisis management and recovery plan—any essential requirements should be incorporated in the plan.

Desk-top exercises are an excellent way to encourage crisis

management teams to further develop the plan and to become more involved in the overall crisis plan.

## FULL-SCALE EXERCISE

This is the big one. The full-scale exercise will involve most of the activities related to the transfer of knowledge from the plan. This is very much like the real thing. The objective is to improve the effectiveness of those responsible for crisis management at every level, at the same time as giving the team the chance to test all aspects of their support systems.

The full-scale exercise takes the simulation away from the desk-top and puts it into a more realistic field setting. Instead of presenting the simulation to the team via handouts, the news of the crisis will arrive from a broad range of channels as it would in the real world. The full-scale exercise can and should happen anytime of the day or night. The exercise will give the team a greater opportunity to test their decision-making skills in a more realistic timeframe. On the one hand, the team will have more time to deal with the problem, but on the other hand, a lot more will happen at all times of the event. This will be a more stressful experience than the desk-top exercise. Team members will have to make decisions at every stage of the crisis escalation and resolution.

There are many different ways of producing a full-scale exercise. Selecting the scenario is the key. If you are an oil company or a large industrial organisation, you would aim at testing the extent of your crisis planning across land, sea and air.

In the case of a major oil spill at sea, a full-scale exercise would test the emergency response capability of the oil spill control clean-up, as well as shareholder response should the event have a detrimental effect on the environment. Teams would be tested at each location.

In the case of a resource or mining company, it may be an under-ground accident at a distant location where rescue and emergency teams would work with locational crisis management teams to deal with the problems, particularly if there were injuries. At the same time, there would be a crisis team at the head office of the mining company dealing with the business issues related to a shut-down or loss of operations at that site and the effect that may have on the future of the business.

A full-scale exercise for a manufacturing company could involve a product recall across three countries, where crisis management teams in each country have to deal with a threat to the future of the brand, the reputation of the parent company and a collapse of share price. Teams in each country would have to co-ordinate information to employees, customers, government, investors and so on. International time zones would be factored in to put the response under greater pressure.

Whatever the scenario, and whatever the business, the exercise has to put the participants under a large amount of pressure, in order to maximise the response effort.

## Planning and organising

The full-scale exercise, if conducted effectively, will be a great asset to the crisis management planning process. It will refine and put into context the written plan. It places the crisis management team, as the most important corporate resource, into a situation where they have to integrate internal human and technical resources in order to solve their problem.

But a good simulation, while taking up valuable time and effort, should not bring the business to a standstill or stop production, nor should it put at risk the lives of teams and employees. Full-scale exercises need to be planned in co-ordination with occupational health and safety standards. Work needs to start some months beforehand. Some of the larger oil companies, when testing their facilities and capabilities to respond to a major explosion or spill, take many months to set up the crisis scenario.

Because this full-scale exercise will be particularly focused on involving the team interaction with outside stakeholders, extensive planning has to go into putting the scenario into the right context. For example, the organisers of a full-scale exercise may deliberately choose an event that will test the crisis team in handling the emotional problems from a fatal incident, with families of victims actually having to face the team in a live confrontation. At the same time, members of the team may face financial analysts, brokers and bankers who are challenging them on the falling share price.

How long should a full-scale exercise take? Some run over days. Army, navy and air force exercises have been known to run for weeks. However, most exercises should take from one to two days in order to expose the team to a realistic timeframe of events and an extensive post-evaluation.

The facilitators will decide, according to the nature of business and the scenario, a timeframe that will reflect similar pressures of a real event. Practically, the scenario should take place at an unusual hour rather than from 9.00 a.m. to 5.00 p.m. so that at least the crisis team and its technical and human support systems are given the toughest test.

A full-scale exercise will require a specific project budget and a dedicated project team to manage the event. In planning the budget, it is important that facilitators take into consideration the extensive time spent by staff assisting in the planning. It is a relatively easy task to budget for specific consultants' time, project managers' time, role players, camera operators, actors and the hire of equipment, but it is often forgotten that the setting time can involve many other management and employees' hours. Time can be the most expensive cost over-run.

As mentioned in the section on desk-top exercises, it is essential for these interactive simulations to be performed on home ground. To take a crisis team away from their most likely setting and test them with perfect equipment and ideal support is not putting them under pressure or simulating what may happen when systems collapse or support teams fail to respond.

For an exercise to be an actual learning experience, facilitators will need to be present wherever the crisis team is providing response actions. If the human resources and family co-ordinator is assisting employees, then a facilitator should review the actions. If the team leader goes to a special room to brief the chief executive and the chairperson, then a facilitator should be there. If the emergency services and security co-ordinator spends time briefing the police and paramedics, then the facilitator should be reviewing that response.

Ideally, the organisation should invest in a video of the whole crisis exercise and debrief. While the lessons from any full-scale exercise will be extensively catalogued and incorporated in the plan, a video provides an on-the-spot record of what people actually said and did. A video record of the highlights of the scenario can be edited to a useful crisis simulation training tool.

## Steps in designing and conducting a full-scale exercise

- Determine the key organisational objectives for the exercise.
- Decide whether it will test one team or more.
- Decide who will facilitate and manage the project (internal or external or a combination of both).
- Set up a critical path.
- Develop a scenario.
- Pre-test scenario through workshop meetings with operational personnel.
- Adjust scenario and gain CEO approval.

- Review project and scenario with emergency services and safety management.
- Gain approval from outside authorities, police, fire, etc.
- Write scripts for role players.
- Brief the facility.
- Test communication equipment.
- Decide on delivery points of scenario to the team.
- Conduct the exercise. Facilitate information on crisis to team.
- Conclude exercise.
- Meet with all players and team immediately for short debrief and cool down.
- Break to allow facilitators to compare information and set up structure for critique and evaluation.
- Conduct full debrief. All team members, including role players and some support teams as well as receptionists, telephonists, security, etc.
- Facilitators prepare debrief report and recommendations.

As mentioned earlier, an exercise may only involve one team and the necessary support and role players, however should the exercise expand to include other crisis teams in other locations, each team should debrief at its own location at first. When each team has carried out the necessary review, critique and evaluation of their response, a full debrief of all teams should take place as soon as possible after the event. This is where critical elements of communication between teams and support staff will be conducted and valuable lessons identified. The group debrief can be carried out by transporting all teams to one central location or by using telephone or videoconferencing techniques.

Rely on crisis management exercises to give you a constructive insight into your organisation's response capability. More importantly, a full-scale exercise will test the little things that could bring a response effort down—it will test the communication systems rigorously and it will analyse the flow of information to essential stakeholders. A full-scale exercise will provide the pre-crisis planning element of closing the gaps in the crisis management plan. It will signal ways to minimise future problems.

A final word of warning. Full-scale exercises involve many people and a lot of equipment in a very stressful and realistic situation. Pressure and strain can lead to injury, and therefore the greatest care and concern should be given to the safety and security of those involved. Confidentiality of the scenario is an important factor in maintaining organisational security.

## CONTROL POINTS

- ☐ Crisis-prone organisations are vulnerable and need continual review and testing of plans.

- ☐ Once individual team role players have worked through typical scenarios, they will understand what to do when it happens.

- ☐ Where the CEO is available for crisis training purposes, the organisation can be assured of a committed result from all concerned.

- ☐ Conducting training programs away from the actual office location or site does not provide efficient results.

- ☐ Training must include support teams, contractors and other suppliers who may be involved in a typical response.

- ☐ A crisis workshop identifies the team roles and responsibilities, the threats and typical responses and involves people in the crisis process.

- ☐ A desk-top exercise simulates a possible crisis event around the table to build strong, flexible and versatile team thinking.

- ☐ A full-scale exercise is aimed at replicating a real event to test the teams at every level.

- ☐ Rely on crisis management workshops and exercises to give constructive insight into your response capability.

- ☐ Training exercises will provide information to close the gaps and make your plans more seamless.

# 12

## THE CRISIS HIT LIST—WHAT TO DO WHEN IT HAPPENS

### CRISIS CONTROL—ACTION CHECKLIST

When crisis strikes, there is no time to waste fumbling through pages of documents. Keep it simple and develop action checklists from your master plan and manuals. Your fast response could help a serious situation from becoming even worse. With simple checklists like the one below, you can create an audit trail of essential actions for every team member. Also see Figure 12.1 for an effective crisis control model.

**Before a crisis**
- ☐ Identify threats
- ☐ Develop crisis team
- ☐ Create crisis plan and rehearse

**During a crisis**
- ☐ Activate team and log events
- ☐ Confirm facts and notify head office
- ☐ Control switchboard and reception
- ☐ Establish your message agenda
- ☐ Advise employees and community
- ☐ Only one spokesperson to brief media
- ☐ Recover operations

**After a crisis**
- ☐ Debrief stakeholders
- ☐ Counsel those affected
- ☐ Run business resumption strategy

**Media interviews**
- ☐ Decide on five key points
- ☐ Control the agenda based on those points

- [ ] Select a positive location
- [ ] Project confidence
- [ ] Begin with human issues
- [ ] Eliminate industry jargon
- [ ] Don't apportion blame
- [ ] Maintain eye contact
- [ ] Don't restate negative questions
- [ ] Start and finish on a positive note

*Figure 12.1 Crisis control model*

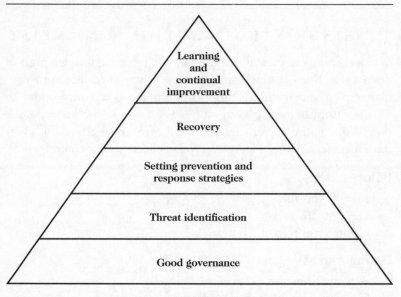

## CONTROL POINTS

- [ ] Getting ahead of the crisis agenda calls for a solid crisis planning model based on strong corporate governance to give authority and depth to the process.

- [ ] Understanding the threats at every site, location and office allows crisis prevention and response strategies to be identified and planned.

- [ ] Crisis recovery must be planned well in advance.

- [ ] Ongoing learning and continual improvement will keep the process current and reliable.

# INDEX